BUSINESS
ENGLISH

비즈니스 실무영어

성태수 지음

신아사

성태수
한국외국어대학교 영어학 박사
현 남서울대학교 글로벌지역문화학과 영미문화전공 교수

비즈니스 실무영어

초판 1쇄 발행 _ 2018년 2월 28일

저　자 · 성 태 수
발행인 · 정 현 걸
발　행 · 신 아 사
인　쇄 · 토탈프로세스
주　소 · 서울특별시 은평구 통일로 59길 4 (2층)
전　화 · (02) 382-6411　팩스 · (02) 382-6401
홈페이지 · www.shinasa.co.kr
E-mail · shinasa@daum.net
출판등록 · 1956년 1월 5일 (제 9-52호)

ISBN 978-89-8396-257-7(13740)

정가 14,000원

머리말

이 책은 영어를 공부하면서도 정작 영문 서신을 쓸 때 큰 부담을 느끼는 이들에게 도움이 되는 내용을 담고 있습니다. 저자는 이런 모습을 주변에서 자주 목격했고, 그 후로 무역관련 서신에 관심을 갖고 관련된 유용한 자료를 모으기 시작했습니다. 또 몇 년 전부터 학교에서 실무영어라는 강좌를 맡으면서 영문 무역서신을 좀 더 손쉽게 쓸 수 있는 방법이 없을까를 고심하게 되었습니다. 다행히 이전부터 여기저기에서 영문서신 자료를 모아오던 터라 내친 김에 책을 써 내려가기 시작했습니다.

우선 이 책은 무역서신 연습서로서 서신 작성의 목적과 작성 방법 등을 서술하고 있으며, 취업 관련 영문 취업지원서, 영문이력서, 영문추천서 작성법을 설명을 담고 있으며, 해외 무역에 필요한 거래처 문의, 신용조회 요청, 거래제의 및 상품구매 조회, 대리점 계약 의뢰, 주문품 통지 및 독촉서신, 상품 훼손 및 수량부족 관련 서신, 방문계획 등의 서신 내용을 포함하고 있습니다.

이 책의 내용은 무역이나 경영에 대한 지식이 부족하더라도 누구나가 영문 무역서신에 쉽게 접근할 수 있게 꾸며졌으며, 특히 스스로 영문 서신 형식을 이해하고 실제로 서신을 작성하는 데 큰 도움이 되리라 기대됩니다. 누구나가 이 책에 제시된 서신 작성에 필요한 적절한 표현과 예제를 기초로 하여 무역절차에 따른 무역서신 작성을 연습할 수 있습니다.

이 책이 개인적인 관심이나 혹은 무역영어 강의를 통하여 많은 사람들에게 소개되고 이 소개된 내용이 많은 사람들에게 유용한 정보로 사용되기를 고대하며, 무엇보다 신아사 관계자 분들에게 감사의 말씀을 전합니다.

성산골에서 성태수 지음

목차

I. 무역서신 작성 요령

II. 취업관련 서류(양식작성 요령)

III. 무역서신 연습

I

무역서신
작성 요령

무역서신 (작성 요령 및 내용)

무역서신은 고객에게 어떤 새로운 서비스를 제공한다든지 거래에 대한 요청이나 제안, 확인 등을 목적으로 한다.

1. 무역서신을 쓸 때 유의할 점

1단계) 서신 목적을 생각하자.

서신 내용은 발신자가 의도를 정확히 포함해야 하고, 수신자에게 서신 내용이 효과적으로 전달할 수 있어야 한다. 무역서신에서 작성자는 수신자가 자신을 해당 직무에서 최고로 인식하도록 신경 써야 한다.

2단계) 서신 작성 내용을 먼저 노트한다.

중요한 내용을 빠뜨리지 않도록 전달할 내용을 사전에 노트해 보는 것이 매우 중요하다.

3단계) 오류를 점검하고 불필요한 내용은 삭제한다.

무역서신은 정확한 정보만을 포함해야 한다. 불필요한 수식어나 반복되거나 상관 없는 내용이 있는지를 살펴보아야 한다.

2. 무역서신의 구성

무역서신의 목적과 내용이 결정되면 전달하고자 하는 전체 내용을 세 부분으로 나눌 수 있다. 도입부분(opening paragraphs), 내용전달부분(middle paragraphs), 마무리부분(closing paragraphs) 각각의 내용을 살펴보자.

1) 도입부분 (opening paragraphs)

도입 부분은 전달하고자 하는 내용의 주제를 밝혀준다. 회신일 경우 이전 서신에 대한 정보를 언급해준다.

I am writing to inform you that we have enclosed the price list and some samples
Thank you for your letter of April 1, inquiring about our product.
Further to your letter of April 1, we are delighted to introduce our product.

2) 내용 전달 부분

내용 전달 부분은 구체적이고 논리적이며 모든 관련 사항을 포함해야 한다. 서신을 통해 여러 가지 내용을 전달해야 하는 경우 문단(paragraphs) 사용이 필수적이다. 한 문단은 10-15줄 정도가 무난하다. 문단 앞에 번호를 매기는 경우도 있다.

3) 마무리 부분

마무리 부분은 도입 부분에서 제시된 내용을 수신자에게 재확인시켜준다. 주요 내용을 반복하거나 사후 조치에 대해 설명과 함께 정중히 마무리한다.

Again we regret the delay in the delivery of your three-piece suite.
We will inform our agents in USA which are interested in this kind of business.
We look forward to receiving your reply as soon as possible.
We look forward to hearing from you soon.
Please feel free to contact me if you have any any questions.

참고 무역서신의 예

Amherst, Inc East 55 Lexington Avenue, Manhattan, New York, NY10050 phone:(212)556-1234/ Fax:(212)556-1235/ mandmco@finance.com	레터헤드(Letter Head)
Your ref: A-1 Our ref: 65	참조번호(Reference Line)
March 30, 2017	날짜(Date)
DMS Korea, Inc. 321 Myoung-dong, Chung-ku Seoul 130-040, Korea Phone: 82-2-570-2121 Fax: 82-2-570-2122	수신자 주소(Inside Adress)
For the attention of Mr. MIN-SHIK CHUNG	특정 수신자 표시 (Attention Line)
Dear Sirs,	첫인사(Salutation)
RE: DEEP SEA DIVING WATCHES	주제표시(Subject Line)

We are interested in the PRD-22 deep sea diving watch which you had on display at the Seoul Trade Fair last week.

We should be grateful if you could give us a quotation for 150 of these. Please also let us know your terms of payment and how quickly you can despatch the goods.

You may be interested to know that we are one of the largest importers of electrical products in Hongkong. As we are trying to extend our range of goods, we are always looking for products of quality and reliability.

We look forward to hearing from you soon.

Yours faithfully,	끝인사(Complementary Close)
Amherst, INC.	발신자 회사이름 (Company Name)
Signature ________ Don Slobin Manager	서명(Signature)
CPC/MT	발신담당자 식별표시 (Identification Marks)
Enc. catalogue	동봉물 표시(Enclosure)
C.C.-Executive managers	사본 송부처 표시(Carbon opy)
P.S. Some of our managers will visit Singapore on business next week.	추신(Postscript)

3. 서신 구성요소의 배열(layout)

- 서신 구성요소들의 위치는 미국, 영국 혹은 개인, 회사의 취향에 따라 다양하다.
- 표준서신양식은 크게 네 개의 부분으로 나누어진다.

1) 머리 부분(Heading)

a. 레터헤드(Letter head)

- 무역서신의 레터헤드는 회사의 로고, 이름, 주소, 전화번호, 텔렉스 혹은 e-mail주소를 포함한다.

b. 참조번호 (Reference Line)

- 레터헤드는 '참조번호' 항목을 포함할 수 있다.

예) Your ref: your ref: 65

- 회신을 보낼 때 'Our ref'에 있는 번호를 'Your ref'에 써넣어야 한다. 이 참고번호는 수신한 회사 측에서 쉽게 내용과 관련된 그들의 이전 서신을 찾는데 도움을 준다.
- '참조번호'란에는 숫자, 부서 이름, 담당자 이름, 서류명 등을 적어 넣을 수 있다.

c. 날짜 (Date)

- 레터헤드는 날짜를 포함할 수 있다. 그러나 레터헤드 아래 부분(왼쪽 혹은 오른쪽)에 직접 타이핑하는 것이 관례이다.

예) 영국식: 5 June 2017
미국식: June 5, 2017

- 무역서신에서 연도나 달을 생략하지 않는 것이 좋으며 ('98, Aug.), 날짜는 기수, 서수 모두가 상관없으나 읽을 경우에는 서수로 읽어야 한다. 끝자리가 '1', '2', '3'일 경우는 'th' 대신 다음과 같이 표기한다: 21st, 22nd, 23rd

예) August 20, 2017
20th August 2017

2) 도입부(Preliminaries)

서신 본론을 쓰기에 앞서 서신 주제를 간단히 밝힌다.

a. 수신자 주소 (Inside Address)

- 인사말(salutation)에 수신자의 이름이 들어갈 경우는 수신자 주소에도 수신자의 이름이 필요하다. Mr, Mrs, Ms 등의 표현을 꼭 필요하다.

예) Mr. P. Kayne
Mr. Desmond John

- 무역서신은 아래 예에서와 같이 직함 사용하는 것이 좋다.

예) Mrs. Joan Johnson
Executive Director
Community Corporation
346 Elm Street
Madison, SD 57042
United States

- 영국에서는 'Mr.' 대신 'Esq.'를 쓰기도 한다.

예) P.R. Brown Esq 혹은 Mr. P.R. Brown

- 발신인이 정민식씨 집에 세들어 살 경우는 c/o MIN-SHIK CHUNG 으로 쓴다. c/o는 care of 의 약어이다.

b. 특정수신자 표시(Attention Line)

- 서신 내용과 가장 밀접한 관계가 있는 사람이나 특정 부서로 서신을 보낼 때 사용한다.

- 이 표시를 통해 담당자가 부재 시 직무를 담당할 적임자를 지정할 수 있다.

- 밑줄이나 대문자를 사용한다.

예) ATTENTION: Mr. MIN-SHIK CHUNG
ATTN: Mr. MIN-SHIK CHUNG
For the attention of Mr. MIN-SHIK CHUNG

c. 첫인사(Salutation)

- 첫인사는 Dear 혹은 My dear로 시작하며, 호칭은 서신을 주고받는 이들의 관계에 따라 다르다. Dear 뒤에는 성이나 이름만을 쓰고, 성명 전체를 쓰지는 않는다.

예)

	수신자 주소	첫인사
회사 이름만 아는 경우	Global Enterprises	Dear Sirs,
수신자 직위만 아는 경우	The Manager	Dear Sir,
수신자가 여성인 경우	The Personnel Officer	Dear Madam,
이름 알고 공식적일 경우	Mr. Richard A. Chaco	Dear Sir,
이름 알고 비공식적일 경우	Mr. Richard A. Chaco	Dear Mr. Chaco,
이름 알고 여성일 경우	Ms. Jane Austin	Dear Ms. Austin,
개인적이고 친밀한 경우	Ms. Jane Austin	Dear Jane,

참고

부서 이름	
Finance Department	재정부
Research and Development Department	연구개발부
Personnel Department	인사부
General Affairs Department	총무부
Public Relations Department	홍보부
Overseas Operation Department	해외사업부
Marketing Department	제조판매부
Engineering Department	기술부
Sales Department	영업부
Accounting Department	경리부
Secretarial Department	비서실
Division	부서/지부
Affiliate	지부/계열회사

직함	
Chairman	회장
President	사장
Vice-president	부사장
Executive Managing Director	전무
Executive Director/ Managing Director	상무
Director	이사
Representative Director	대표이사
Manager	부장/지배인
General Manager	총지배인
Assistant Manager	차장
Branch Manager	지점장
Section Chief	과장
Staff	직원
Representative	주재원

줄임말		
Co.	Company	회사
Corp.	Corporation	(법인)회사
Inc.	Incorporated	주식회사(미국)
Ltd.	Limited	주식회사(영국)
Bldg.	Building	건물
Dept.	Department	부서

d. 주제 표시(Subject Line)

- 주제 표시(Subject Line)는 서신 내용에 앞서 미리 주제를 밝힌다. 본문의 첫 문단의 내용이 주제 표시를 대체할 수 있다. 주제 표시 방법은 다음과 같다.

예) Re: RICOH FT 4030 COPIERS
RE: RICOH FT 4030 COPIERS
SUBJECT: RICOH FT 4030 COPIERS
RICOH FT 4030 COPIERS

3) 마무리 부분(Signing Off)

서신 내용을 마치고 발신자를 재확인시킨다.

a. 끝인사(Complementary Close)

예) Yours sincerely,
(Very) sincerely yours,
Sincerely,
With kind regards,
Best regards,
Best wishes,
Thanks,
Wishes

b. 회사 이름(Company Name)

- 회사 이름은 끝인사 바로 밑에 대문자로 쓴다.

예) Yours sincerely,
(for) Amherst, INC.

c. 발신담당자 식별 표시(Identification Marks)

- 발신자 이름의 이니셜은 대문자로 쓰고, 그 뒤에 타이피스트나 비서 이름의 이니셜을 대문자나 소문자로 적는다.

예) CPC/mt
CPC/MT
CPC-mt

d. 동봉물 표시(Enclosures)

- 계약서, 캐달로그, 송장 등을 서신과 동봉할 때 사용하는 표시이다.

예) Enc. 2 Bills of Lading
Encl(s). 1 Invoice
Enclosures: 1 Price list
1 Order form

e. 사본 송부처 표시(Carbon Copy)

- 서신 사본을 참고로 그 밖의 다른 곳으로 보내야 할 경우 사용된다.
- 'bcc'는 'blind carbon copy'를 의미하는데, 이는 또 다른 사본이 수신자이외의 다른 사람에게 보내진 사실을 수신자에게 밝히지 않기 위해 사용한다.
- 수신자가 받는 사본에는 'bcc'를 타이핑하지 않는다.

예) cc Exotic Hotel
CC: Mr. Richard Kayne, L.A. Branch
Carbon copy to Director

4) 추신(Postscript)

- 서신 작성 후 새로운 내용을 추가할 경우 사용된다.

예) PS or P.S.

5) 레이아웃의 종류 (Layout Styles)

- 레이아웃과 관련하여 주의할 점은 다음과 같다.

a) 문단을 시작할 때 인덴트(indent)를 줄 경우 대무분의 워드프로그램에 인텐트 기능을 이용할 수 있다. 인덴트 기능을 사용하지 않은 경우 영어는 space bar를 2, 4, 6번씩 치고 내용을 치며, 한국어는 주로 한 음절이 space bar 2번에 해당하므로 2번을 치고 내용을 친다.
b) 행을 바꿔어 분철(syllabification)을 해야할 경우 분리되는 단어 뒤에 hypen(-)을 붙이고, 행을 바꾼다.

분철이 가능한 경우는 a) 음절 사이(sin-cere), b) 동일한 자음이 겹칠 때(hap-py), c) 접사와 어간 사이(un-happy)이다.
분철이 불가능한 경우는 a) 1음절 단어, b) 사람 이름(*Da-vid)이나 금액(*$20,0-00)을 표시하는 경우이다.

a. 완전 수직형(Fully Blocked Style)

Amherst, Inc
East 55 Lexington Avenue, Manhattan, New York, NY10050
phone:(212)556-1234/ Fax:(212)556-1235/ mandmco@finance.com

DMS Korea Co., Inc.
321 Myoung-dong, Chung-ku
Seoul 130-040, Korea
Phone: 02-570-2121
Fax: 02-570-2122

Dear Sir,

DEEP SEA DIVING WATCHES

We are interested in the PRD-22 deep sea diving watch which you had on display at the British Trade Fair last week.

We should be grateful if you could give us a quotation for 150 of these. Please also let us know your terms of payment and how quickly you can dispatch the goods.

You may be interested to know that we are one of the largest importers of electrical products in the U.S. As we are trying to extend our range of goods, we are always looking for products of quality and reliability.

We look forward to hearing from you soon.
Sincerely yours,

signature

____

Don Slobin
Manager

b. 수직형(Blocked Style)

Amherst, Inc
East 55 Lexington Avenue, Manhattan, New York, NY10050
phone:(212)556-1234/ Fax:(212)556-1235/ mandmco@finance.com

DMS Korea Co., Inc.
321 Myoung-dong, Chung-ku
Seoul 130-040, Korea
Phone: 02-570-2121
Fax: 02-570-2122

Dear Sir,

DEEP SEA DIVING WATCHES

We are interested in the PRD-22 deep sea diving watch which you had on display at the British Trade Fair last week.

We should be grateful if you could give us a quotation for 150 of these. Please also let us know your terms of payment and how quickly you can dispatch the goods.

You may be interested to know that we are one of the largest importers of electrical products in the U.S. As we are trying to extend our range of goods, we are always looking for products of quality and reliability.

We look forward to hearing from you soon.

Sincerely yours,

signature

Don Slobin
Manager

c. 부분 들여쓰기형(Semi-Indented Style)

Amherst, Inc

East 55 Lexington Avenue, Manhattan, New York, NY10050

phone:(212)556-1234/ Fax:(212)556-1235/ mandmco@finance.com

DMS Korea Co., Inc.
321 Myoung-dong, Chung-ku
Seoul 130-040, Korea
Phone: 02-570-2121
Fax: 02-570-2122

Dear Sir,

DEEP SEA DIVING WATCHES

We are interested in the PRD-22 deep sea diving watch which you had on display at the British Trade Fair last week.

We should be grateful if you could give us a quotation for 150 of these. Please also let us know your terms of payment and how quickly you can dispatch the goods.

You may be interested to know that we are one of the largest importers of electrical products in the U.S. As we are trying to extend our range of goods, we are always looking for products of quality and reliability.

We look forward to hearing from you soon.

Sincerely yours,

signature

____

Don Slobin
Manager

d. 완전 들여쓰기형(Fully Indented Style)

Amherst, Inc
East 55 Lexington Avenue, Manhattan, New York, NY10050
phone:(212)556-1234/ Fax:(212)556-1235/

DMS Korea Co., Inc.
321 Myoung-dong, Chung-ku
Seoul 130-040, Korea
Phone: 02-570-2121
Fax: 02-570-2122

Dear Sir,

DEEP SEA DIVING WATCHES

We are interested in the PRD-22 deep sea diving watch which you had on display at the British Trade Fair last week.

We should be grateful if you could give us a quotation for 150 of these. Please also let us know your terms of payment and how quickly you can despatch the goods.

You may be interested to know that we are one of the largest importers of electrical products in the U.S. As we are trying to extend our range of goods, we are always looking for products of quality and reliability.

We look forward to hearing from you soon.

Sincerely yours,

signature

Don Slobin
Manager

6) 봉투(Envelope)

- 서신 레이아웃이 봉투에도 그대로 적용된다.

① 봉투와 편지지에 있는 이름, 직위, 주소 등을 일치시킨다.
② 봉투와 편지지의 레이아웃을 일치시킨다.
③ 서신 내용에 특정 수신자 표시(attention line)가 있을 경우는 봉투에도 적는다.
④ 육상이나 해상우편은 surface mail, 항공우편은 air mail이라 하고 봉투왼쪽 밑에 표시한다.
⑤ 반송을 의뢰를 원할 경우는 발신인 주소 밑에 'If not delivered, please return to the sender.'가 인쇄된 봉투를 사용할 수 있다.

<봉투>

a. 수직형 봉투쓰기(Blocked Layout)

Amherst, Inc.
East 55 Lexington Avenue
Manhattan, New York, NY10050

VIA AIR MAIL

<u>For the attention of Mr. MIN-SHIK CHUNG</u>

DMS Korea Co., Inc.
#1602, 16 Fl. DaeRyung Bldg.
321 Jungang-ro, Guro-ku
Seoul 08240, Korea

Private and Confidential

b. 들여쓰기 봉투쓰기 (Indented Layout)

Amherst, Inc.
East 55 Lexington Avenue
Manhattan, New York, NY10050

VIA AIR MAIL

<u>For the attention of Mr. MIN-SHIK CHUNG</u>

DMS Korea Co., Inc.
#1602, 16 Fl. DaeRyung Bldg.
321 Jungang-ro, Guro-ku
Seoul 08240, Korea

Private and Confidential

비즈니스 실무영어

II

취업관련 서류
(양식작성 요령)

1. 취업 지원서 (The letter of Application)

1단계: 광고를 잘 참고한다.
2단계: 자격요건과 경험을 언급한다.
3단계: 그 직업에 대한 자신의 지식을 언급한다.
4단계: 구체적인 일과 관련된 경험을 언급한다.
5단계: 회사에 기여할 수 있는 여타의 경력과 자신의 가치를 언급한다.
6단계: 자신이 기대하는 급여를 언급한다. (상대방에서 물을 경우에만)
7단계: 동봉하는 서류를 언급한다. (이력서, 프로필서신, 자격증사본, 사진 등)
8단계: 면접에 대해 언급한다.

구인 광고기사 (Wanted Advertisment))

Laboratory Technician Wanted

An established international petroleum Engineering Service company invites applications for the position of: Laboratory Technician

Incumbent will be required to carry out analysis of reservoir fluid samples.

Requirements:

1. Polytechnic diploma in chemical process technology preferred.
2. 'A' level certificate holder in Science or technical subjects may also apply.
3. Analytical and willing to learn
4. Experience not necessary as training will be provided.

Interested candidates please write by April 10, 2017 with your full resume, current and expected salary, contact number and non-returnable photograph to:

The Advertiser
Good Nature Co., Inc.
321 Myoung-dong, Chung-ku
Seoul 130-040, Korea
Phone 02-570-2121
Fax: 02-570-2122

(구직지원 서신)

구직서신은 권유서신(solicited letter)와 비권유서신(unsolicited letter)가 있다. 회사에 보내지는 권유서신은 구인광고를 기초로 하며, 비권유서신은 구인광고 없이도 발신인 임의로 작성된다.

Sample letter 1

#102-1501, Samik Apt.
Daebang-dong, Dongjak-gu
Seoul 100-789, Korea
+82-2-3451-0890(h)/+82-10-3204-2961(C)
summi@dreamsearchkorea.com
April 5, 2017

The Advertiser
Good Nature Co., Inc.
321 Myoung-dong, Chung-ku
Seoul 130-040, Korea
Phone: 02-570-2121
Fax: 02-570-2122

Dear Sir,

RE: POST of LABORATORY TECHNICIAN

I wish to be considered for the post of Laboratory Technician advertised in the Korea Herald of 2 April 2017. My formal training at Hankook University, together with nearly two months of industrial training, has provided me with the experience and skills required for this post.

I have just completed a degree course in Chemical Process Technology at Hankook University where, in addition to theoretical knowledge in subjects learnt the techniques necessary in analysing samples. During the industrial orientation programme I was able to apply my theoretical knowledge to a practical situation. As an assistant to the chemical engineer I analysed the metal content in the solution used for the printed circuit board. This practical experience enabled me to realize that I have an aptitude for, as well as an interest in, the analysis of samples.

On Monday evening I am commencing a 10-week computer course because I believe that the skills to be gained from it will be an asset in any employment I take up in the future.

As a university student I would expect a starting salary in the range of $1500-$2000 per month. I am enclosing a photograph and full resume for your information. If you require any further details I am available for an interview at your convenience.

Enthusiastically,

signature
SEUNG JOO LEE (Mr.)

Enc. 1 resume

Sample letter 2

3456 Massachusetts Ave., NW
Washington, DC 20016-8104
777-777-7777
address@gmail.com
March 7. 2017

Ms. Mary McCloud
Officer Manager
Global Fund for Women
1234 Sutter Street, Suite 400
San Francisco, CA 94109
United States

Dear Ms. McCloud,

As a graduating senior in American University's School of International Service, I have developed a focus on gender and development. Since I have a keen interest in the Global Fund for Woman and completely support its mission to advance women's human rights, I am applying for the Development Fellow for Individual Giving position posted on your Web site.

During my intership at the Central American Resource Center in Washington, DC, I gained experience working in the development office of a nonprofit. Interning in the fast-paced work environment strengthened my organizational skills and my ability to manage several tasks simultaneously. I completed an extensive investigatin of potential public and private funders to the organization through phone calls and internet research. After determining whether or not our organization met the funder's criteria, I wrote letters of inquiry to obtain their support. In completing these tasks I developed strong professional written communication skills while working to meet deadlines.

I gained additional experience in international issues during my recent internship at Amnesty International' s Women's Human Rights Program. I created five fact sheets, compiled 50 articles for a monthly on-line bulletin seen by 600 subscribers, and composed ten sample letters for the on-line action network. I also fielded calls and responded to emails from a diverse group of Amnesty members who requested informatin about the Women's Human Rights Program.

I have enclosed my resume. If you have any questions or need additional information, please contact me at 777-777-7777 or by email at address@gmail.com. I am available to start work on May 15. Thank you for your time and consideration. I look forward to hearing from you.

Sincerely,

(signature)
Jane Austin
enclosure(s)

2. 이력서 (Resume, 'ray-zoo-may'로 발음)

이력서는 경력이나 자격과 같은 개인적 신상기록이다. 영국에서는 'curriculum vitae' (C.V.) 라고 불린다. 이력서의 레이아웃은 지원자의 개성을 반영한다. 아래 Ms. Sung-Won Lee와 Mr. Sung-Jin Kim의 이력서 예를 보자. 그녀는 연구기술원 자리에 지원하고 있다.

예제 이력서 1

RESUME

Sung-Won Lee
Samik Apt. 102-1501,
Daebang-Dong, Dongjak-Gu
Seoul 100-789, Korea
+82-2-3451-0890 / +82-18-3204-2961
sungwon@korea.com

PERSONAL

	Birth Date	February 9, 1982
	Sex	Female
	Marital Status	Single

OBJECTIVE A position in the field of marketing, sales management, trading, buying or related affairs in a multinational company.

EDUCATION

7/2009 - 5/2010	**ECC LANGUAGE SCHOOL** Seoul, Korea Completed AFKN Listening course and English Conversation Program.
12/2005 - 2/2006	**SAMSUNG TRADING CO., LTD** Seoul, Korea Completed extensive training courses of Presentation Techniques.

3/2002 –2/2006	**HANKOOK UNIVERSITY** Seoul, Korea Bachelor of Arts in Political Science and Diplomacy, College of Social Science. GPA 3.88/4.5 *Recipient of merit based scholarship. *Passed qualifying examination to study in Japan held by the University in 1995.
3/2004 - 6/2005	**SDS LANGUAGE INSTITUTE** Seoul, Korea Completed intensive Japanese Conversation Course up to Level 5 out of 6.

EXPERIENCE

3/2007 - Present	JAYU COMPANY Seoul, Korea Assistant Manager - Trading & Distribution Dept. *Responsible for overall import & export activities of the distribution company specializing in optical communication materials for network systems. *In charge of domestic buying affairs in domestic market. *Managed and controlled accounts' sales target and result to provide full business support.

ADDITIONAL

Languages
Fluent in written and spoken English & Japanese.

Computer
Proficient in Excel. Well-versed in MS-Word, PowerPoint, Inter-net.

Extra
* Vice President, Netsgo English Club.
* Interests include Internet surfing, films, music, swimming, traveling, etc.

7/2005 - 2/2007	**SAMSUNG TRADING CO., LTD.** Seoul, Korea Associate - Sales & Marketing Team (December 1995 - February 1997) Internship(July 1995 - December 1995)

REFERENCES Available upon request.

예제 이력서 2

Curriculum Vitae

Kim, Sung-Jin
733-4 Mia-dong, Sungbuk-ku
Seoul 120-234, Korea
(02)978-2673
KSJ@hotmail.com

Educational Background
Graduated from the above University with a B.A. degree in English in August 2008.
Entered the Department of English at Hankook University in March 2003. Seoul, Korea.
Graduated from Korea High School in 2002. Seoul, Korea.

Military Service
Discharged from the ROK Army in March 2006.
Enlisted in the ROK Army in August 2003.

Honors and Prizes
Graduated from Hankook University with distinction in August 2008.
Awarded a prize in an intercollegiate English contest in May 2007.
Received a merit-based scholarship from Hankook University from 2002 to 2003.

Activities
Member of Christian Campus Crusade at Hankook University from 1992 to 2008.
Member of Kangnam Taekwondo Club from 2002 to present.
Lab Assistant for the Department of English, Hankook University in 2002.

References
Dr. Park, Su-Jeen
Associate Professor
Dept. of English, Hankook University
Seoul, Korea
+82-2-922-3333

Dr. Kim, Kyu-Shik
Assistant Professor
Dept. of English, Hankook University
Seoul, Korea
+82-2-922-3334

3. 커버레터 및 추천서

일부 회사나 관공서는 취업지원양식을 요구한다. 다음은 작성 시 주의 사항이다.

a. 원서를 기입하기 전에 지시사항을 정확히 숙지한다.

Write in BLOCK CAPITALS.
Write in black ink.

b. 깨끗한 작성이 좋은 인상을 준다. 수정을 피하기 위해 미래 작성해본다.

c. 빈칸을 남기지 않는다. 해당 없음은 'N/A' (Not Applicable) 혹은 None으로 쓴다.

d. 전화번호나 단어철자들이 정확한지 확인한다.

지원서에 첨부되는 서신의 예

#102-1501 Samik Apt.
211 Daebang-dong, Dongjak-gu
Seoul 100-789, Korea
+82-2-3451-0890
sungwon@korea.com

March 12, 2016

Dear Sir,

Clerical Officer II

I am enclosing the completed application form for the post of Clerical Officer II as advertised in the Korea Herald of March 8.

Although I have been working for only a year, now I become familiar with both Photo shop and CAD. In addition, I have attended a 3-day word processing course, thus enabling me to make use of a word processor's full range of functions.

My typing speed is 45 wpm and I believe I am capable of the appointment as Grade II Clerical Officer.

Sincerely

(Signature)
Sung-Won Lee

(해석) 2급 사무직원

코리아헤롤드 3월 8일자에 광고 되었듯이 2급사무직을 위한 지원서를 작성해 동봉합니다. 단지 1년 직장생활을 했지만 포토샵과 CAD에 매우 익숙합니다. 더욱이 3일간 워드프로세서 강좌를 수강하고 모든 워드프로세서 기능을 활용할 수 있게 되었습니다. 타이핑속도는 1분에 45단어(words per minute)를 치며 2급사무직에 채용될 수 있음을 믿습니다.

예제 추천서 1

TO WHOM IT MAY CONCERN:

RE: MR SEUNG-JOO LEE

I have known MR. Seung-Joo Lee since he first started at the Hankook University. As his English professor, I have been greatly impressed by his degree of competence in expressing himself both orally and in writing. No doubt his ability as a communicator has been further developed by being on the executive committee of the Catholic society during his second year at the University.

Although he is a fine communicator, Seung-Joo Lee has other, more important qualities. He is always cooperative and friendly, being willing to help other students in the class, yet also relating well to his lecturers. As a student he has matured considerably during his time at the University. He now fully appreciates the need to work hard and his attitude to his studies is commendable. He is very conscientious and puts all his efforts into whatever he is doing.

From what I know of him, I believe Seung-Joo Lee would make an excellent employee in view of his pleasant personality and his willingness to commit himself to the job-in-hand.

Sincerely,

(signature)
CHEONG-HUN LEE
Professor
English Language Department
Hankook University
Tel: 02-879-3383

예제 추천서 2

December 6, 2015

To whom it may concern

YOUNG-TAI LEE

I have known Young Tai for three and a half years. He has been a faithful employee of Jackie's Kitchen Korea Co., Ltd. since it first commenced on 12 April 2002. For your information, Jackie's Kitchen is a franchise restaurant involving Jackie Chan, the movie star (see www.jkkorea.co.kr).

Young-Tai has been responsible for many aspects in the preparation and opening of the Jackie's Kitchen restaurant in Korea. These include organizing restaurant uniforms, crockery, menu design, procurement and management of hall staff, training and store promotional activities. He has been instrumental in opening 4 restaurants to date and there are already 2 further restaurants planned in the next 4 months of which he will be an integral part.

Young-Tai joined the Company with little experience but has progressed much faster than expected and has shown talent for developing a restaurant from scratch. Much of what is currently seen at the restaurants is Young-Tai's initiatives. He is diligent and has good common sense which I believe is the most important qualities from an employer's perspective. He has been a significant asset to the Company. However, he needs to further develop his organizational skills which will come from experience and managing staff underneath him.

I would recommend him highly for any position in the food and beverage or service industry.

If you would like to contact me, please call me at +82-2 302-8090.

Sincerely yours ,

Sang-Jin Hong
CEO

비즈니스 실무영어

III
무역서신 연습

1. 시장조사 (Market Research)

- 수출업자는 상품을 수출하기 위해서는 해외시장조사를 통해 목표시장을 선정하고 잠재 고객을 파악해 한다. 다음과 같은 절차를 따른다.

  a. 우선 상품을 매매할 시장을 찾는다.

  b. 수출하는 상품이 과연 수출 대상국에서 수요 가능성이 있는지 판단한다.

  c. 수출 대상국의 소비자나 기업가 필요로 하는지를 판단한다.

  d. 거래처 현지 시장의 정치적 경제적 상태나 항만, 운송시설을 살펴본다.

  e. 수출 과정에서 경쟁 제품이 유무를 살피고, 거래 유망성을 판단한다.

  f. 수출 대상국이 자국의 산업 보호를 위한 통관 절차나 수입 규제를 행하고 있는지를 살펴본다.

이 과정에서 직접 현지를 방문하는 자체조사 외에 해외 거래처에 대한 정보를 의뢰할 수 있는 기관은 내외 상공회의소나 거래국의 공관, 또 거래은행이나 상사, 영사관, 대한무역협회, 대한무역진흥공사, 관련조사기관이다. 관련기관으로는 Dun and Bradstreet Corp.가 유명하다. 이들을 통해 위탁조사를 할 수 있다.

(참고) 무역거래절차도 (신용장 결제방식)

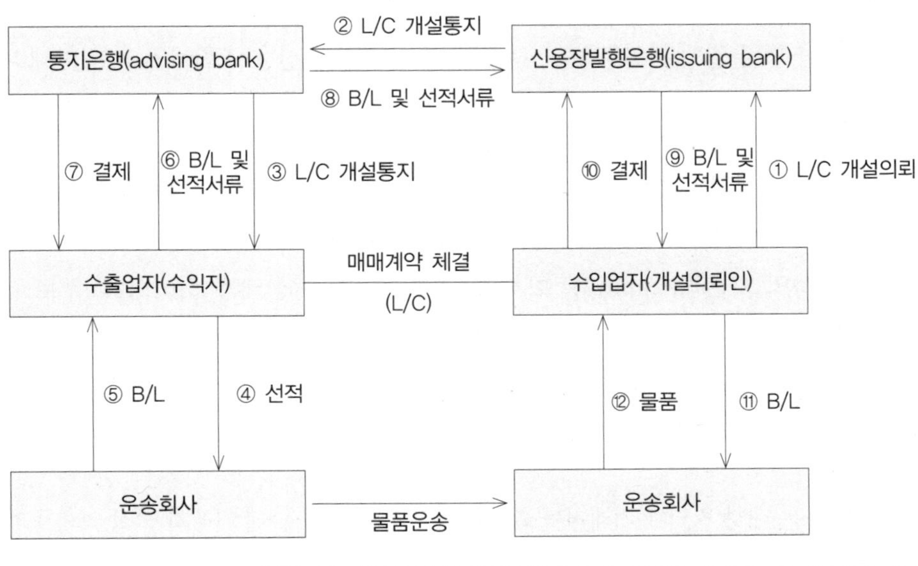

2. 거래처 선정 방법

(참고) 거래처 선정 방법

- 인터넷(Alibaba, EC21, ECPlaza, Tpage, BuyKorea 등)
- 무역디렉토리(KOMPASS, Thomas Register, American Export, Ward's Business 등)
- 상공회의소
- 무역박람회
- 대한무역협회
- 무역관련잡지
- 대사관
- 영사관
- 대한무역투자진흥공사
- 현지시찰
- 컨설팅회사
- 거래처
- 거래은행
- 현지주재원

거래처 선정

- 거래처 선정 의뢰 시 유의점

시장 조사를 마치고 적절한 거래처를 선정한다. 거래처에 대한 엄격한 신용조회는 매우 중요하다. 무역 거래는 신용을 바탕으로 이루어지므로, 거래처 신용 상태가 불량할 경우 상품 인수 회피나 대금 결제 지연과 같은 문제의 소지가 있다. 신용 조회에 필요한 아래 내용을 3C's 라고 부른다.

a. 회사의 성격(Character): 계약 이행에 대한 성실성, 평판, 업무 태도, 채무 이행에 대한 성의, 대금 결제의 확실성, 경영진의 품격 등을 고려한다.

b. 회사의 자본력(Capital): 회사의 전반적인 재정 상태를 의미하며, 주로 대차대조표(B/S: Balance of Sheet)와 관련되는 사항을 조사한다.

c. 회사의 영업 능력(Capacity): 영업 능력이 없으면 훌륭한 재무 상태에서도 회사의 발전 가능성을 희박하다.

수출업자는 대상 지역에 거래처를 확보하기 위해 여러 기관에 거래처 선정 의뢰를 할 수 있다.

3. 거래처 선정 의뢰 서신

내용

1) 자회사를 소개하고, 해당 기관에 거래처 추천을 의뢰하는 서신의 주제를 밝힌다.
2) 자회사의 신용 조회처를 밝힌다.
3) 회신을 부탁한다

표현연습

1) 자회사를 소개하고, 해당 기관에 거래처 추천을 의뢰하는 서신의 주제를 밝힌다.

a) We are writing to inform you that we are scheduled to expand the amount of business we do with the U.S. and would be obliged if you could provide us with a list of reliable companies in your area.
(당사는 미국과 거래를 확대할 계획입니다. 신용할 만한 회사를 소개해 주십시오.)

b) We are writing to ask you to introduce us to any importers who are interested in this line of business. We are exporting televisions, and now planning to do business with the most reliable firms in the U.S. We should be glad if you could introduce us to any importers who are interested in this line of business.
(이 계통의 무역에 관심있는 수입업체를 당사에 소개해 주실 것을 요청드립니다. 당사는 텔레비전을 수출하고 있고 현재 귀하의 나라의 신뢰할 만한 회사와 거래를 할 계획입니다.)

2) 자회사의 신용 조회처를 밝힌다.

a) For information concerning our credit standing, we can refer you to City Bank, Inc., 253 Myoung-dong, Seoul.
(본 회사의 신용 상태에 대하여 시티은행에 조회해 보십시오.)

b) As our banker, City Bank, Inc., 253 Myoung-dong, Seoul, will supply necessary information on our financial standing or credit standing for you.
(당사의 거래 은행인 시티은행 서울지점에서 재정 상태나 신용 상태에 대한 필요한 정보를 제공할 것이다.)

c) Our banker is City Bank, Inc., 253 Myoung-dong, Seoul, from whom you can get all the information you need on our financial standing.
(당사의 거래 은행인 시티은행 서울지점이 당사의 재정 상태에 관한 필요한 모든 정보를 드릴 것입니다.)

3) 회신을 부탁한다.

a) We are looking forward to receiving your reply as soon as possible.
(가능한 빠른 회신을 고대합니다.)

Sample letter

Good Nature Co., Inc.

321 Myoung-dong, Chung-gu, Seoul 130-040, Korea

Phone 02-570-2121/ Fax: 02-570-2122/ Email: Goodnaturekorea@Korea.com

March 25, 2016

Mr. Dan Slobin
President
Inter-American Development Bank
229 West 43rd Street
New York, NY 10036
Phone: 212-556-1234
Fax: 212-556-1235

Dear Sir,

We are pleased to inform you that our firm is exporting televisions, and now planning to do business with the most reliable firms in your country. We hope that you will introduce us to any importers who are interested in this line of business.

As to our credit standing and financial standing, we can refer you to City Bank, Inc., 253 Myoung-dong, Seoul, and the Chamber of Commerce.

We look forward to receiving your reply as soon as possible.

Sincerely yours,

singnature

____

MIN-SHIK CHUNG
Manager

(해석)

당사는 텔레비전 수출업체이고 현재 귀하의 나라의 신뢰할 만한 업체와 거래를 모색하고 있습니다. 이 계통의 무역에 관심이 있는 수입업체를 소개해 주시면 감사하겠습니다. 당사의 신용 상태나 재정 상태에 대해서는 시티은행 서울지점이나 상공회의소에 조회해 주십시오. 조속한 회신을 고대합니다.

Sample letter

Good Nature Co., Inc.

321 Myoung-dong, Chung-gu, Seoul 130-040, Korea

Phone 02-570-2121/ Fax: 02-570-2122/ Email: Goodnaturekorea@Korea.com

January 15, 2016

The Chamber of Commerce
of the State of Iowa
65 Jefferson Avenue, Iowa city, IO10005
U.S.A.

Gentlemen:

For the last two decades, we have been supplying all kinds of electric machines to our domestic market and also to various markets abroad enjoying a good reputation.

Now we hope to extend our business to your market and shall be much obliged if you introduce us to some reliable firms in your city who are interested in this line of business.

As to our credit standing, the Bank of Japan, Ltd. will supply necessary information.
We appreciate your consideration in advance and wait for your early reply.

Yours very truly,

signature

____

MIN-SHIK CHUNG
Export Manager

(해석)

당사는 지난 20년간 국내에서 또 해외시장에 전자기계를 공급해 좋은 명성을 누리고 있습니다. 지금 귀하는 시장으로 거래를 확대하려고 합니다. 이런 종류의 무역에 관심이 있는 귀하는 도시에 있는 몇몇 신뢰할 수 있는 회사를 저희에게 소개를 해주시면 감사하겠습니다. 당사의 신용상태에 대하선 일본은행이 필요한 정보를 드릴 겁니다. 미리 귀사의 배려 에 감사드리며 조속한 회신을 기다립니다.

참고. 거래처 선정 의뢰 회신

The Chamber of Commerce of the State Iowa
65 Jefferson Avenue, Iowa city, IO10005, U.S.A.

Good Nature Co., Inc.
321 Myoung-dong, Chung-gu
Seoul 130-040, Korea
Phone: 02-570-2121
Fax: 02-570-2122

January 15, 2016

Dear Sirs,

Thank you for your letter of February 20, inquiring about sales distributors for your products.

We confirm that we have forwarded your letter to the following companies who will contact you directly:

1) Actimail, Inc., 875 Avenue of the Americas Suite 1107, New Yor, NY 10001, United States
2) Cummings Advertising, 5301 East Street, Ste. 212, Rockford, IL 61108, United States

We hope that this will help you.

Sincerely yours,

(signature)
Richard Taylor
Corporate Section

4. 신용조회 의뢰(Credit Inquiry) 서신

수출/수입업체는 상대가 지정한 신용 조회처를 통해 상대 업체의 신용상태를 조회한다.

내용
1) 신용 조회 의뢰에 대한 주제를 밝힌다.
2) 의뢰하고자 하는 내용을 밝힌다.
3) 내용에 대한 비공개를 언급한다.

표현연습

1) 신용 조회 의뢰에 대한 주제를 밝힌다.

a) DMB Korea Co., Inc. 321 Myoung-dong, Chung-ku, Seoul 130-040, Korea, has named you as a credit reference.
(DMB Korea는 귀사를 신용조회처로 지명했습니다.)

b) Your bank was referred to us as a trade reference by DMB Korea Co., Inc., 321 Myoung-dong, Chung-ku, Seoul 130-040, Korea, interested in exporting their products.
(제품을 수출하고자 하는 DMS Korea는 귀 은행을 신용조회처로 지명했습니다.)

2) 의뢰하고자 하는 내용을 밝힌다.

a) We should be obliged if you could let us know the financial standing of Amherst, Inc., East 55 Lexington Avenue, Manhattan, New York, NY10050.
(Amhert회사의 재정 상태를 알려주십시오.)

b) We shall appreciate it if you inform us of information on this firm, including their credit and financial standing.
(회사의 신용 상태, 재정 상태를 포함한 정보를 알려주세요.)

3) 내용에 대한 비공개를 언급한다.

a) Any information you may give us will be treated in strict confidence.
(귀사가 제공한 모든 정보를 극비로 다루어질 것이다.)

b) Whatever data you may give us will be treated confidentially.
(귀사가 제공하는 모든 자료는 극비로 다루어질 것이다.)

Sample letter 1

Amherst, Inc
East 55 Lexington Avenue, Manhattan, New York, NY10050
phone:(212)556-1234/ Fax:(212)556-1235/ mandmco@finance.com

The American First Bank
22 Liberty Street
New York, NY10045
(212)720-2144

Dear Sirs,

DMS Korea Co., Inc., 321 Myoung-dong, Chung-ku, Seoul 130-040, Korea, has named you as a credit reference.

We shall appreciate it if you inform us of information on this firm, including their credit standing and financial standing.

Any information you may give us will be treated in strict confidence.

Sincerely,

signature

____

Dan Slobin
Manager

Sample letter 2

Amherst, Inc
East 55 Lexington Avenue, Manhattan, New York, NY10050
phone:(212)556-1234/ Fax:(212)556-1235/ mandmco@finance.com

The American First Bank
22 Liberty Street
New York, NY10045
(212)720-2144

Dear Sirs,

Your bank was referred to us as a reference by DMS Korea Co., Inc., 321 Myoung-dong, Chung-ku, Seoul 130-040, Korea, who hopes to export their products.

We should be obliged if you could let us know the financial standing of DMS Korea Co., Inc. Whatever you may give us will be held confidential.

We look forward to your prompt reply.

Sincerely,

signature

____

Dan Slobin
Manager

(참고) 무역서신에서 많이 쓰이는 동사표

acomplish, achieve	:	달성하다	act	:	활동하다
adapt	:	적용하다	administer	:	관리하다
analyze	:	분석하다	arrange	:	준비하다
assemble	:	모으다	attain	:	획득하다
audit	:	회계감사하다	automate	:	자동화하다
balance	:	비교평가하다	budget	:	예산을 세우다
calculate	:	계산, 산정하다	clarify	:	명백하게하다
classify	:	분류하다	comply	:	편집하다
complete	:	완료하다	compute	:	산정하다
conceptualize	:	개념화하다	conduct	:	행동, 안내하다
consolidate	:	합병하다	contract	:	계약하다
contribute to	:	공헌하다	control	:	통제,감독하다
coordinate	:	조정하다	counsel	:	상담하다
delegate	:	파견하다, 위임하다	demonstrate	:	설명, 시범하다
design	:	고안, 설계하다	develope	:	개발하다
diagnose	:	진단하다	direct	:	지도하다
dispatch	:	파견, 급파하다	diversify	:	다양화하다
educate	:	교육하다	eliminate	:	제거하다
enable	:	가능하게하다	encourage	:	촉진하다
engineer	:	공사감독을 맡다	establish	:	설립하다
evaluate	:	평가하다	execute	:	수행하다
facilitate	:	용이하게하다	familiarize	:	활성화하다
focus	:	집중하다	forecast	:	예측하다
formulate	:	공식화하다	found	:	창설하다
generate	:	초래하다	guide	:	지도하다
identify	:	증명하다	illustrate	:	설명하다
implement	:	이행하다	improve	:	개선하다
influence	:	영향을주다	initiate	:	시작하다
innovate	:	혁신하다	inspect	:	조사하다
install	:	설치하다	instruct	:	가르치다
integrate	:	통합하다	interpret	:	해석하다
introduce	:	소개, 도입하다	investigate	:	조사하다
launch	:	시작, 착수하다	maintain	:	유지하다
manage	:	관리하다	monitor	:	관찰, 감독하다
motivate	:	동기부여하다	negotiate	:	협상하다
operate	:	작동, 관리하다	organize	:	조직하다
perform	:	수행하다	persuade	:	설득하다

plan	:	계획하다	prepare	:	준비하다
produce	:	생산하다	program	:	계획짜다
project	:	계획하다	promote	:	촉진, 홍보하다
recommend	:	추천하다	recruit	:	모집하다, 채용하다
reduce	:	감소하다	repair	:	보수하다
research	:	연구, 조사하다	restore	:	복구하다
restructure	:	재구성하다	review	:	재조사하다
revitalize	:	활성화하다	schedule	:	계획을 짜다
screen	:	심사하다	shape	:	구체화하다
skill	:	숙련하다	solidify	:	구체화하다
specify	:	명확히하다	stimulate	:	자극, 활기있게하다
strengthen	:	강화하다	summarize	:	요약하다
supervise	:	감독하다	survey	:	조사하다
systematize	:	조직화하다	train	:	훈련하다
translate	:	번역하다	trim	:	다듬다
upgrade	:	개량, 개선하다	validate	:	유효하게하다

5. 신용조회 의뢰 회신

내용

1) 서신수취 확인한다.

2) 의뢰 받은 회사의 신용상태를 언급한다.

3) 맺음말을 한다.

표현연습

1) 서신수취 확인한다.

a) It is our great pleasure that we can answer your letter of March 3, 2017 about Amherst, Inc.
(Amherst, Inc.에 관한 2017년 3월 3일자 귀사의 서신에 회신을 드립니다.)

b) We are writing in connection with your credit inquiry of March 6 about DMS Korea Co., Inc.
(DMS Korea Co., Inc.에 관한 3월 6일자 신용조회와 관련해 글을 드립니다.)

2) 의뢰받은 회사의 신용상태를 언급한다.

a) Amherst, Inc. has been a credit customer of ours for the past 5 years. They have paid his account on time. In addition, they have introduced to us several customers equally reliable.
(Amherst, Inc.은 당사의 지난 5년간 신용거래처이다. 그들은 금액을 정확한 일자에 지불하고 당사에 동일하게 신뢰할 만한 여러 거래처를 소개해왔다.)

b) Although Amherst, Inc. has been a customer of ours, we do not have a sufficient relationship to feel comfortable to vouch for them. We have made shipments to his company twice during the past 2 years. Their payments have been timely. The firm has a good reputation within the trade but we do not have any knowledge of their credit standing.
(Amherst, Inc.이 당사의 거래처지만 그 회사를 편하게 보증할 만한 충분한 관계를 아직 수립하지 못하고 있다. 당사는 지난 2년간 두 번 물품을 배송한 적이 있다. 지불을 제 시기에 이루어졌다. 그 회사는 교역에서 좋은 평판을 가지고 있으나 당사는 그 회사에 대한 신용상태를 잘 파악하지 못하고 있다.)

c) The firm is not under favorable conditions. Probably the firm's difficulties seem to be due to bad management. Consequently, most of the firm's suppliers not only give very short credit for limited sums but make deliveries on a cash basis as well.
(이 회사의 상태는 좋지 않습니다. 아마도 회사의 어려움은 경영에서 기인하는 것 같습니다. 결과적으로 대부분의 공급처들이 제한된 액수에 대한 단기 지불유예기간을 주며 현금거래를 바탕으로 물품을 배송한다.)

3) 맺음말을 한다.

a) We recommend Amherst, Inc. to you with no reservations.
(당사는 Amherst, Inc.을 조건 없이 추천합니다.)

b) I regret that I cannot give you more details about Amherst, Inc.
(Amherst, Inc.에 대한 더 많은 세부사항을 알려드릴 수 없어서 유감입니다.)

c) If you have any questions about Amherst, Inc., please feel free to contact us.
(Amherst, Inc.에 대한 질문이 있으시면 부담 갖지 말고 당사로 연락주세요.)

Sample letter 1

The American First Bank
22 Liberty Street New York, NY10045
(212)720-2144

DMS Korea Co., Inc.
321 Myoung-dong, Chung-ku
Seoul 130-040, Korea
Phone: 02-570-2121
Fax: 02-570-2122

Dear Sirs:

It is our great pleasure that we can answer your letter of March 3, 2006 about Amherst, Inc.

Amherst, Inc. has been a credit customer of ours for the past 5 years. They have always paid his account on time. In addition, they have sent us several customers equally reliable.

We recommend Amherst, Inc. to you with no reservations.

Yours truly,

signature

____

Richard Taylor
Corporate Section

Sample letter 2

The American First Bank
22 Liberty Street New York, NY 10045
(212)720-2144

DMS Korea Co., Inc.
321 Myoung-dong, Chung-ku
Seoul 130-040, Korea
Phone: 02-570-2121
Fax: 02-570-2122

Dear Sirs:

We are writing in connection with your credit inquiry of March 6 about Amherst, Inc.

Although Amherst, Inc. has been a customer of ours, we do not have a sufficient relationship to feel comfortable to vouch for them. We have made shipments to his company twice during the past 2 years. Their payments have been timely. The firm has a good reputation within the trade but we do not have any knowledge of their credit standing.

I regret that I cannot give you more details about Amherst, Inc.

Yours sincerely,

signature

____

Richard Taylor
Corporate Section

6. 거래제의 (Business Proposal)

수출업자가 수입업자에게 거래 가능성을 타진하기 위해 보내는 서신이다. 예상거래처가 결정되면 거래를 제안하는 서신과 자사의 캐달로그를 발송한다. 이때 상대회사에 자회사의 좋은 심어주는 것이 중요하다. 또 구매를 유도하기 위한 흥미 있는 내용도 필수적이다. 거래제의 서신은 상대회사를 알게 된 경위, 자회사 경영규모와 상태, 취급 품목, 대금결제 방법 등을 내용으로 담아야 한다.

내용

1) 상대회사를 알게 된 경위를 밝힌다.
2) 당사의 제품을 소개한다.
3) 제품에 대한 확신을 심어준다.
4) 당사의 신용조회처를 알려준다.
5) 동봉물을 밝히고, 회신을 요청한다.

표현연습

1) 상대회사를 알게 된 경위를 밝힌다.

a) Your name has been recommended to us by City Bank, Seoul Branch, and we are writing to you with a desire to do business with you.
(소개를 통해 연결된 경우: 시티은행 서울지점이 귀사를 추천했고, 귀사와 거래하기를 바랍니다.)

b) We learned form the Seoul Trade Fair that you are looking for our Model 221 printer.
(무역박람회를 통해 연결된 경우: 서울무역박람회에서 귀사가 모델 221형 프린터기를 찾고 계심을 알았습니다.)

c) We learned much about your company in the March 7, 2006 of Korea Herald.
(신문이나 잡지에서 알게 된 경우: 2006년 3월 7일자 코리아헤롤드에서 귀사를 알게 되었습니다.)

2) 당사의 제품을 소개한다.

a) We would like to introduce our product of the latest model in wide use all over the world.
(전세계적을 널리 사용되고 있는 당사의 최신 모델을 소개합니다.)

b) This model is scheduled to be released on May 2006.
(이 모델은 2006년 5월에 출시될 예정입니다.)

c) This product has several improvements and on competitors in quality and accuracy.
(이 제품은 여러 가지 품질 향상을 행해졌고 품질과 정확도에서 경쟁상대가 없습니다.)

3) 제품에 대한 확신을 심어준다.

a) We are sure that our product will meet your exact requirements.
(당사의 제품은 틀림없이 귀사의 정확한 요구조건을 만족시킬 것입니다.)

b) We assure you that our product would meet both market and customer needs.
(당사의 제품은 틀림없이 시장과 고객의 욕구를 만족시킬 것입니다.)

c) You are assured that you will be satisfied with the product's high quality and reasonable price.
(제품의 높은 질과 합리적인 가격에 만족하실 것입니다.)

4) 당사의 신용조회처를 알려준다.

a) As to our credit standing, we can refer you to City Bank, Seoul Branch, and the Chamber of Commerce.
(신용조회처로서 시티은행 서울지점과 상공회의소가 당사의 신용상태를 알려드릴 것입니다.)

b) As our banker, City Bank, Seoul Branch, will supply necessary information.
(당사의 거래 은행인 시티은행 서울지점이 필요하신 정보를 제공할 것입니다.)

5) 동봉물을 밝히고, 회신을 요청한다.

a) We have enclosed a catalog and a price list. If you would like to have further information, please contact us.
(캐달로그와 가격목록을 동봉합니다. 더 많은 정보를 원하신다면 당사로 연락주세요.)

b) Specifications are enclosed. If you have any questions, please let us know.
(질문이 있으시다면 연락주세요.)

c) I am looking forward to hearing from you.
(회신을 고대합니다.)

d) I hope that you will be interested in our product.
(당사의 제품에 관심이 있으시길 바랍니다.)

Sample letter 1

DMS Korea

DMS Korea Co., Inc.
321 Myoung-dong, Chung-ku, Seoul 130-040, Korea
Phone 02-570-2121/ Fax: 02-570-2122/ Email: Goodnaturekorea@Korea.com

Amherst, Inc.
East 55 Lexington Avenue
Manhattan, New York, NY10050.
phone:(212)556-1234
Fax:(212)556-1235

Dear Sirs,

Your name has been recommended to us by City Bank, Seoul Branch, and we are writing to you with a desire to do business with you.

We would like to introduce our television of the latest model in wide use all over the world. We are confident that our product will meet your exact requirements.

Our banker is City Bank, Seoul Branch, from whom you can get all the information you need on our financial standing.

I have enclosed a catalog. If you would like to have further information, please contact us at 82-2-570-2121. I hope that you will be interested in our products.

Sincerely,

Signature

____

MIN-SHIK CHUNG
Manager

Sample letter 2

DMS Korea

DMS Korea Co., Inc.

321 Myoung-dong, Chung-ku, Seoul 130-040, Korea

Phone: 02-570-2121/ Fax: 02-570-2122/ Email: Goodnaturekorea@Korea.com

Amherst, Inc.
East 55 Lexington Avenue
Manhattan, New York, NY10050.
phone:(212)556-1234
Fax:(212)556-1235

Dear Sirs,

We learned about your company from the March issue of Business Week. We are pleased to inform you that we have recently developed a new home running machine called the Model 221 Techno-Run.

This machine has all the features of our professional gym model, costing less than a half price. We are sure that you will be satisfied with its outstanding performance.

A product catalog is enclosed. If you need more details, please let us know. We look forward to receiving your reply.

Sincerely yours,

signature

____

MIN-SHIK CHUNG
Manager

Writing Practice

당사는 몇 일전 귀사의 홈페이지를 방문하였고, 귀사 업무성격과 여러 취급 품목에 관심을 갖게 되었습니다. 당사는 한국의 일류 가정용 전자제품 제조업체로 내년에 신제품 출시를 예정하고 있습니다. 새로 출시될 Model 221은 귀사 및 고객들의 요구에 부응하리라 생각합니다. 당사는 미국에서 그 제품을 판매하기를 원하며 판매거래처를 찾고 있습니다. 캐달로그 한부를 동봉합니다. 귀사의 신속한 회신을 고대합니다.

7. 조회(inquiry) 서신

조회란 수입업자 입장에서 거래 관계의 제안에 대해 좀 더 구체적인 거래조건을 보내달라고 요청하거나, 거래 관계의 권유나 제안 없이 수입업자가 먼저 오퍼를 보내 달라고 요청하는 것이다. 조회서신은 물품거래의 직접적인 내용을 다룬다는 점에서 실질적인 무역거래의 시작이다. 상품구매 전 상품 견본, 가격, 공급수량, 출하가능 시기 등의 내용을 문의한다.

내용

1) 상대회사를 알게 된 경위를 밝힌다.
2) 제품의 정보, 견본, 견적 등을 요청한다.
3) 회신을 요청한다.

표현연습

1) 상대회사를 알게 된 경위를 밝힌다.

a) We noticed the Model 221 printer in the February 2006 issue of Business Week.
(비지니스위크 2006년 2월호에서 모델221 프리터기를 보았습니다.)

b) We read about your advertisement in the Korea Herald of March 2, 2006 and am very interested in your product. We are sure that your product will be most suitable for our market.
(2006년 3월 2일자 코리아헤롤드에서 귀사의 광고를 읽었고, 귀사 제품에 관심을 갖게 되었습니다. 귀사 제품은 이곳 시장에 가장 적합할 것이라 확신합니다.)

c) Thank you very much for your letter of May 5, 2006, introducing the new Model 221 printer to us.
(신형 모델 221 프린터기를 소개해 주신 2006년 5월 5일자 서신에 감사드립니다.)

2) 제품의 정보, 견본, 견적 등을 요청한다.

a) Would you please send us a price list by airmail or fax?
(항공우편이나 팩스로 가격목록을 보내주십시오.)

b) Please could you send us a brochure and a quotation.
(소개 책자나 견적서를 보내주세요.)

c) We would be grateful if you could send us the quotation for 10 units and specification of your product.
(제품 10개에 대한 견적서와 제품 사양을 보내주세요.)

3) 회신을 요청한다.

a) We are looking forward to hearing from you soon.
(조속한 회신을 고대합니다.)

b) We appreciate your proposal and look forward to your early response.
(귀사의 제의에 감사드리며, 빠른 회신을 고대합니다.)

Sample letter 1

Amherst, Inc
East 55 Lexington Avenue, Manhattan, New York, NY10050.
phone:(212)556-1234/ Fax:(212)556-1235/ mandmco@finance.com

DMS Korea Co., Inc.
321 Myoung-dong, Chung-ku
Seoul 130-040, Korea
Phone: 02-570-2121
Fax: 02-570-2122

Dear Sir,

Thank you very much for your letter of May 5, 2017, introducing the new Model 221 printer, which we are now considering purchasing.

Please could you send us the latest product catalog and a quotation.

We are looking forward to hearing from you.

Sincerely yours,

signature

____
DAN SLOBIN
Manager

Sample letter 2

Amherst, Inc
East 55 Lexington Avenue, Manhattan, New York, NY10050.
phone:(212)556-1234/ Fax:(212)556-1235/ mandmco@finance.com

DMS Korea Co., Inc.
321 Myoung-dong, Chung-ku
Seoul 130-040, Korea
Phone: 02-570-2121
Fax: 02-570-2122

Dear Sir,

We noticed your Model 221 in the February 2017 issue of Business Week. We are very much interested in this product. We are confident that your product is most suitable for our market.

Would you please send us the following information:
- Unit price
- Discount information
- Delivery time
- Availability of stock
- Payment terms

We look forward to your early reply.

Sincerely yours,

signature

____
DAN SLOBIN
Manager

Writing Practice

귀사 여성용 의류를 소개해주신 2016년 3월 20일자 서신에 감사드립니다. 당사는 귀사의 제품에 많은 관심이 있습니다. 다음 달 말까지 1000벌의 여성용 의류에 대한 견적을 보내주십시오. 1000벌 이상의 주문에 대해 수량할인이 가능한지를 알고 싶습니다. 조속한 회신을 부탁드립니다.

8. 조회 회신

내용

1) 서신 수취를 확인해 준다.
2) 조회 내용에 대한 답변을 준다.
3) 재고의 유무 혹은 지불방법 등을 구체적으로 언급한다.
4) 맺음말을 한다.

표현연습

1) 서신 수취를 확인해 준다.

a) Thank you very much for inquiring about our products.
(당사의 제품을 조회해 주셔서 감사드립니다.)

b) Thank you very much for your letter of March 14, inquiring about a quotation of our products.
(당사 제품의 견적을 요청하신 3월 14일자 서신에 감사드립니다.)

2) 조회 내용에 대한 답변을 준다.

a) We are sending a price list and two product samples to you.
(가격목록과 두 개의 견본을 보내드립니다.)

b) We are sending you a quotation and a discount rate of our product separately.
(견적서와 할인율을 별도로 보내드립니다.)

3) 재고의 유무 혹은 지불방법 등을 구체적으로 언급한다.

a) We have the products in stock. The products are currently available.
(현재 재고가 있고 이들은 이용 가능합니다.)

b) We will ship the products immediately after receiving your order.
(당사는 주문을 수취한 후 바로 제품을 선적하겠습니다.)

c) We will be able to ship the products 3 weeks after receiving you order.
(당사는 주문을 수취한 수 3주후에 제품을 선적하겠습니다.)

d) We accept cash or credit card for payment. Please send payment to the following bank account:
City Bank
Bank Account Number: 234-4567-35556
DMS Korea
(당사는 현금이나 신용카드로 결제합니다. 아래 계좌로 입금시켜주십시오.)

4) 맺음말을 한다.

a) If you need further information, please let us know.
(정보가 더 필요하시면, 당사로 연락주세요.)

b) If you have any questions, please feel free to contact us.
(문의사항이 있으시면, 당사로 편하게 연락주세요.)

Sample letter 1

DMS Korea

DMS Korea Co., Inc.
321 Myoung-dong, Chung-ku, Seoul 130-040, Korea
Phone: 02-570-2121/ Fax: 02-570-2122/ Email: Goodnaturekorea@Korea.com

Amherst, Inc.
East 55 Lexington Avenue
Manhattan, New York, NY10050.
phone:(212)556-1234
Fax:(212)556-1235

Dear Sirs,

Thank you very much for inquiring about our product.

We are sending a quotation on Model 221 along with the payment terms. We hope that the price is satisfactory. We will be able to ship the product a week after receiving your order.

If you need more details, please let us know.

Sincerely yours,

signature

____

MIN-SHIK CHUNG
Manager

Sample letter 1

DMS Korea

DMS Korea Co., Inc.
321 Myoung-dong, Chung-ku, Seoul 130-040, Korea
Phone: 02-570-2121/ Fax: 02-570-2122/ Email: Goodnaturekorea@Korea.com

Amherst, Inc.
East 55 Lexington Avenue
Manhattan, New York, NY10050.
phone:(212)556-1234
Fax:(212)556-1235

Dear Sirs,

We are pleased to receive your inquiry of March 15 about our Television.

We inform you of our following payment terms. For orders over $5,000, we ask you to open a letter of credit. For orders under this amount, we prefer credit card or cash payment.

If you have more questions, please feel free to contact us.

Sincerely,

signature

____

MIN-SHIK CHUNG
Manager

Writing Practice

당사 제품의 견적을 요청하신 3월 14일자 서신에 감사드립니다. 가격목록과 두 개의 견본을 보내드립니다. 현재 재고가 있고 이들은 이용 가능합니다. 당사는 주문을 수취한 수 3주후에 제품을 선적하겠습니다. 문의사항이 있으시면, 당사로 편하게 연락주세요.

9. 조회내용 변경요청 서신

내용
1) 서신 수취를 확인한다. 2) 조회 내용에 대한 문제점을 알린다. 3) 문제 해결책을 제시한다. 4) 맺음말을 한다.

표현연습

1) 서신 수취를 확인한다.

a) Thank you very much for your letter of March 14, inquiring about our product.
(당사 제품을 조회해 주신 3월 14일자 서신에 감사드립니다.)

b) We are writing to reply to your letter of March 14, asking for our product.
(당사 제품을 조회해 주신 3월 14일자 귀사의 서신에 대한 회신을 드립니다.)

2) 조회 내용에 대한 문제점을 알린다.

a) Unfortunately, this product is out of stock at the moment.
(유감스럽게도 이 제품이 현재 품절중입니다.)

b) We are sorry to inform you that this product has been discontinued since 2015.
(이 제품은 2015년부터 생산이 중간된 상태입니다.)

3) 문제 해결책을 제시한다.

a) We would like to recommend another product, instead.
(대신 다른 제품을 추천합니다.)

b) We are sending a catalog along with a substitute.
(대체품과 함께 캐탈로그를 보내드립니다.)

4) 맺음말을 한다.

a) I am looking forward to hearing from you.
(회신을 고대합니다.)

b) I hope you find it interesting, and look forward to receiving your message soon.
(귀사에 흥미가 있기를 바라며, 회신을 고대합니다.)

Sample letter 1

DMS Korea

DMS Korea Co., Inc.
321 Myoung-dong, Chung-ku, Seoul 130-040, Korea
Phone: 02-570-2121/ Fax: 02-570-2122/ Email: Goodnaturekorea@Korea.com

Amherst, Inc.
East 55 Lexington Avenue
Manhattan, New York, NY10050.
phone:(212)556-1234
Fax:(212)556-1235

Dear Sirs,

Thank you for your letter of March 14, 2017.

We are sorry to inform you that this product is sold out at the moment. However, a similar product is now available.

We are happy to enclose a price list and a brochure. We look forward to hearing from you.

Sincerely,

signature

____

MIN-SHIK CHUNG
Manager

Sample letter 2

DMS Korea

DMS Korea Co., Inc.
321 Myoung-dong, Chung-ku, Seoul 130-040, Korea
Phone: 02-570-2121/ Fax: 02-570-2122/ Email: Goodnaturekorea@Korea.com

Amherst, Inc.
East 55 Lexington Avenue
Manhattan, New York, NY10050.
phone:(212)556-1234
Fax:(212)556-1235

Dear Sirs,

Thank you for your fax of March 14, 2017, inquiring about our product.

Unfortunately, this product has been discontinued. However, a new model is available, and we are happy to enclose a catalog.

I hope you find it interesting, and look forward to your prompt reply.

Yours sincerely,

signature

____

MIN-SHIK CHUNG
Manager

10. 조회 독촉 서신

조회요청, 선적 기일이 혹은 대금 결제에 대한 독촉 서신 내용이다.

내용

1) 이전 서신 송부를 알린다.
2) 조속한 회신을 요청한다.
3) 이전 서신 사본 한 부를 동봉함을 언급한다.

표현연습

1) 이전 서신 송부를 알린다.

a) We let you know that we sent a letter to you on March 25, but have received no reply yet.
(3월 25일 귀사에 서신을 드렸으나 아직 회신을 받지 못했습니다.)

b) We would like to inform you that we sent a letter to you March 25, asking for a sample. However, I have not heard from you yet.
(견본 요청 서신을 3월 25일에 드렸으나, 아직 회신을 받지 못했습니다.)

c) We are writing with regard to the balance of $10,000 for invoice number ABC-113-23 which was due on March 30. This payment is now four weeks overdue. Our invoice requests full payment in 30 days.
(3월 30일이 기한인 송장번호 ABC-113-23의 잔액 10,000불에 대한 미결제를 통보합니다. 현재 지불기간이 4주가 경과되었습니다. 대금청구서에 따르면 30일내 결제입니다.)

2) 조속한 회신을 요청한다.

a) Would you please answer as soon as possible?
(가능한 빨리 회신을 부탁합니다.)

b) Would you please reply to our letter by April 20?
(4월 20일까지 회신을 보내주십시오.)

c) Hopefully we ask you to settle the balance by April 30.
(4월 30일까지 잔액 결제를 요청합니다.)

3) 이전 서신 사본 한 부를 동봉함을 언급한다.

a) I am sending a copy of our letter to you.
(사본 한 부 우송해 드립니다.)

b) I am enclosing a copy of our letter to you.
(서신 사본 한 부를 동봉합니다.)

c) A copy of our letter is enclosed.
(사본 한 부 동봉합니다.)

Sample letter 1

Amherst, Inc
East 55 Lexington Avenue, Manhattan, New York, NY10050.
phone:(212)556-1234/ Fax:(212)556-1235/ mandmco@finance.com

DMS Korea Co., Inc.
321 Myoung-dong, Chung-ku
Seoul 130-040, Korea
Phone: 02-570-2121
Fax: 02-570-2122

Dear Sirs,

We are writing to inform you that we sent a letter to you on March 25, but have received no reply yet.

Would you please answer as soon as possible?

We are sending a copy of our letter to you.

Sincerely yours,

signature

____

Don Slobin

Manager

Sample letter 2

DMS Korea

DMS Korea Co., Inc.
321 Myoung-dong, Chung-ku, Seoul 130-040, Korea
Phone: 02-570-2121/ Fax: 02-570-2122/ Email: Goodnaturekorea@Korea.com

Amherst, Inc.
East 55 Lexington Avenue
Manhattan, New York, NY10050.
phone:(212)556-1234
Fax:(212)556-1235

Dear Sirs,

We are writing with regard to the balance of $10,000 for invoice number ABC-113-23 which was due on March 30. This payment is now four weeks overdue. Our invoice requests full payment in 30 days.

Hopefully we ask you to settle the balance by April 30.

We are enclosing a copy of our invoice to you.

Sincerely,

signature

____
MIN-SHIK CHUNG
Manager

Writing Practice

당사는 3월 25일자 서신에서 귀사의 모델 322에 대한 견본을 요청한바 있습니다. 그러나 아직 회신을 받지 못하고 있습니다. 이번 달 말까지 견본 하나와 견적서를 보내주십시오. 3월 25일자 서신 사본 한부를 동봉합니다. 조속한 회신을 부탁드립니다.

11. 지사/대리점 요청 서신

내용

1) 시신 수취를 확인해 준다.
2) 거래 회사 제품을 알게 된 경위를 밝힌다.
3) 제품에 대한 시장성을 알려준다.
4) 지사/대리점 요청한다.
5) 자회사를 소개하고, 동봉물 첨부를 알린다.

표현연습

1) 시신 수취를 확인해 준다.

a) Thank you for your letter and product samples of March 14.
(3월 14일 귀사의 서신과 제품 견본에 대해 감사드립니다.)

b) Thank you very much for sending us your product catalog.
(귀사의 제품 캐탈로그를 보내 주셔서 감사드립니다.

2) 거래 회사 제품을 알게 된 경위를 밝힌다.

a) We learned from the March issue of Business Week that you are looking for a sales representative in the U.S.A.
(당사는 귀사가 미국 내 지사모집을 하고 있다는 사실을 비즈니스위 3월호에서 알게 되었습니다.)

b) Mr. Smith told us that at present you have no sales representative in the U.S.A. yet.
(Smith씨께서 귀사가 현재 미국 내 지사가 없다는 사실을 알려 주었습니다.)

3) 제품에 대한 시장성을 알려준다.

a) We have reviewed the information and think that your products might match our market needs.
(제품 정보를 검토해 본 결과, 귀사의 제품이 시장수요에 잘 부합되는 것으로 판단됩니다.)

b) We have evaluated your products and concluded that they would have good market potential in the U.S.A.
(귀사의 제품을 평가한 결과 미국 내에서 훌륭한 시장 잠재력이 있다는 결론을 내렸습니다.)

4) 지사/대리점 요청한다.

a) We would like to distribute your products in the U.S.A.
(미국에서 귀사의 제품을 판매하기를 원합니다.)

b) Would you please let us know if there is any possibility of handling your products in the U.S.A.?
(미국에서 귀사의 제품을 취급할 가능이 있는지를 알려주세요.)

c) Please consider the possibility of our representing your company in the U.S.A.?
(당사의 미국에서 지사를 열 수 있는지를 고려해 주세요.)

5) 자회사를 소개하고, 동봉물 첨부를 알린다.

a) We would like to point out that we specialize in the import of machinery parts.
(당사는 기계부품 전문 수입업체입니다.)

b) We currently have 300 well-organized sales offices around the U.S.A.
(당사는 현재 미국 전역에 300개의 잘 정비된 판매점을 두고 있습니다.)

c) Enclosed is our company profile.
(당사의 소개 책자를 보내드립니다.)

Sample letter 1

Amherst, Inc
East 55 Lexington Avenue, Manhattan, New York, NY10050.
phone:(212)556-1234/ Fax:(212)556-1235/ mandmco@finance.com

DMS Korea Co., Inc.
321 Myoung-dong, Chung-ku
Seoul 130-040, Korea
Phone: 02-570-2121
Fax: 02-570-2122

Dear Sirs,

Thank you very much for sending us your product catalog.

We have reviewed the information and think your products might match our market needs. Do you have any sales distributor in the U.S.A.? If not, would you please consider the possibility of our representing your company?

Enclosed is our company profile. Looking forward to hearing from you soon.

Sincerely yours,

signature

____

Don Slobin
Manager

Sample letter 2

Amherst, Inc
East 55 Lexington Avenue, Manhattan, New York, NY10050.
phone:(212)556-1234/ Fax:(212)556-1235/ mandmco@finance.com

DMS Korea Co., Inc.
321 Myoung-dong, Chung-ku
Seoul 130-040, Korea
Phone: 02-570-2121
Fax: 02-570-2122

Dear Sirs,

Thank you for letter of March 14 and the fabric samples.

After reviewing the samples, we concluded that they would have good market potential in the U.S.A.

We would like to know if you have a sales representative in the U.S.A. Otherwise, would you be interested in representation by our company?

We are pleased to enclose our company profile and look forward to hearing from you.

Sincerely yours,

signature

____

Don Slobin
Manager

Writing Practice

3월 14일 귀사의 서신과 제품 견본에 대해 감사드립니다. 당사는 귀사가 미국 내 지사모집을 하고 있다는 사실을 비즈니스위 3월호에서 알게 되었습니다. 제품 정보를 검토해 본 결과, 귀사의 제품이 시장수요에 잘 부합되는 것으로 판단됩니다. 미국에서 귀사의 제품을 취급할 가능이 있는지를 알려주세요. 당사는 기계부품 전문 수입업체입니다. 당사의 소개 책자를 보내드립니다.

12. 지사/대리점 요청 회신

내용

1) 서신 수취 사실을 확인해 준다.

2) 검토 결과를 통보한다.

3) 다음 일정을 확인한다.

표현연습

1) 서신 수취 사실을 확인해 준다.

a) Thank you very much for your proposal on the sales distribution agreement.
(판매지사 계약에 대한 제의에 감사드립니다.)

b) I appreciate your proposal on the sales plan.
(판매 계획에 대한 귀사 제안에 감사드립니다.)

2) 검토 결과를 통보한다.

(긍정적일 때)

a) We have studied the proposal with much interest and would like to accept it.
(관심을 갖고 제안을 검토해서 제안을 받아들이기로 결정했습니다.)

b) We found the proposal to be very attractive, but would like to discuss it in more detail with you.
(제안에 많은 관심이 있으나 좀 더 구체적인 논의를 갖고 싶습니다.)

c) We would like to have more details on your business terms.
(귀사의 거래 조건에 대해 좀 더 자세한 내용을 알고 싶습니다.)

d) We have some questions about your payment terms.
(귀사의 지불 조건에 대해 몇 가지 질문이 있습니다.)

(부정적일 때)

e) We carefully reviewed your proposal but have decided that we are unable to accept it at this time.

(귀사의 제안을 신중하게 검토했으나 이번에는 수용할 수 없는 것으로 결정했습니다.)

f) The reason is why the budget for next fiscal year has already decided.

(다음 회계연도 예산이 이미 결정되었기 때문입니다.)

g) This is because we have not completed our market research.

(아직 시장조사를 마치지 못했기 때문입니다.)

h) That is why a certain manufacturer produces the same kind of products at lower price.

(다른 제조업체에서 같은 제품을 더 낮은 가격으로 공급하고 있기 때문입니다.)

i) Please keep in touch with us in the future.

(앞으로 계속적인 연락 부탁드립니다.)

3) 다음 일정을 확인한다.

a) Would you please let me know when it would be convenient for us to meet?

(회합의 편리한 날짜를 알려 주세요.)

b) We will inform you as soon as our decision is made.

(결정되는 대로 통보해 드리겠습니다.)

Sample letter 1

DMS Korea

DMS Korea Co., Inc.
321 Myoung-dong, Chung-ku, Seoul 130-040, Korea
Phone: 02-570-2121/ Fax: 02-570-2122/ Email: Goodnaturekorea@Korea.com

Amherst, Inc.
East 55 Lexington Avenue
Manhattan, New York, NY10050.
phone:(212)556-1234
Fax:(212)556-1235

Dear Sirs,

Thank you very much for your proposal on the new business opportunity in your letter of March 25.

We carefully reviewed your proposal but have decided that we are unable to accept it at this time. This is because the market situation is not favorable at present.

However, we hope that we can keep in touch with each other in the future.

Sincerely,
signature

____
MIN-SHIK CHUNG
Export Manager

Sample letter 2

DMS Korea

DMS Korea Co., Inc.
321 Myoung-dong, Chung-ku, Seoul 130-040, Korea
Phone: 02-570-2121/ Fax: 02-570-2122/ Email: Goodnaturekorea@Korea.com

Amherst, Inc.
East 55 Lexington Avenue
Manhattan, New York, NY10050.
phone:(212)556-1234
Fax:(212)556-1235

Dear Sirs,

We appreciate your proposal on the sales distribution agreement.

We studied the proposal and would like to accept it. However, there are still more details we would like to discuss with you.

Would you please let me know when it would be convenient for us to meet? Looking forward to hearing from you soon.

Sincerely,
signature

____

MIN-SHIK CHUNG
Export Manager

Writing Practice

귀사의 판매지사 계약에 대한 제의에 감사드립니다. 제안에 많은 관심이 있으나 좀 더 구체적인 논의를 갖고 싶습니다. 이번 주 말에 미국으로 출장을 계획하고 있습니다. 방문 일정을 통보합니다. 회합의 편리한 날짜를 알려 주세요.

13. 오퍼(청약/제의 : Offer)의 종류

- 오퍼는 일정한 조건 하에서 '계약을 체결'하고 싶다는 의사표시이다.
- 수출업자와 수입업자가 무역계약(contract)을 체결하기까지 한 번의 오퍼가 바로 승낙(acceptance)으로 이어지는 경우도 있지만, 대부분의 계약이 성립되기까지는 여러 교섭(negotiation) 단계가 있다.
- 무업업자들은 반복적인 오퍼를 통해 당사에 유리한 조건을 이끌어내려 노력한다.
- 여러 조건들에 해당하는 구체적 내용은 다음과 같다.

1) 거래 품목(commodity name)
2) 원산지(origin)
3) 규격(specification)
4) 품질(qualilty)
5) 수량(quantity)
6) 단가(unit price)
7) 총가격(amount)
8) 포장(packing)
9) 지불조건(payment terms)
10) 선적지(shipping port)
11) 선적시기/납기일(shipment)
12) 유효기간(validity)
13) 보험(insurance)

여러 오퍼 중에 매도 오퍼(selling offer)가 주를 이루며, 이 오퍼는 조회를 통해 이루어지는 경우도 있고 일방적으로 발생하는 경우도 있다.

13.1 매도오퍼(Selling Offer)와 매수오퍼(Buying Offer)

- 매도오퍼는 수출업자와 매수오퍼는 수입업자와 각각 관련된다.
- 이들은 어떤 특정한 조건으로 물검을 팔고(사고) 싶다는 의사표시로, 상호간의 예상 거래처에서 문의한 내용을 자세하게 답변해주고, 견본 등을 우송해 준다.

- 상품의 견적을 낼 때 상호간의 거래 조건을 명확히 제시하여 사후 문제를 미연에 방지한다.
- 오퍼의 대부분은 매도오퍼이며 정부기관의 입찰공고 등 특정한 경우에 매수오퍼가 있다.

13.2 확정오퍼(Firm Offer: 기한부오퍼)

- 확정오퍼는 가장 전형적인 오퍼로 유효기간(validity)과 선적기일을 명시하고, 상대 회사가 유효기간 내에 회신할 것을 조건으로 하는 오퍼이다.
- 유효기간이 지나면 이 확정오퍼는 실효가 된다.
- 유효기간 내 다른 곳에 오퍼를 하지 못하고, 임의적 변경(amendment), 취소(cancellation), 철회(revocation)가 불가능하다. 상대방이 승낙하면 계약이행의무가 확정된다.
- 이것은 시기적으로 오퍼와 승낙 사이에 가격변동이 예상되는 경우 매우 적절한 오퍼이다. 아래와 같은 문구를 삽입할 수 있다.

예) We offer you firm subject to your acceptance reaching us by June 6, 2017.
We make you a firm offer for delivery by the middle of January at the prices quoted.

내용

1) 확정오퍼를 밝힌다.
2) 오퍼 내용이나 거래 조건을 언급한다.
3) 맺음말을 한다.

표현연습

1) 확정오퍼를 밝힌다.

a) We offer you firm for the following items subject to reply reaching here by noon on September 15.
(9월 15일 정오까지 귀사 회신 당사도착 조건부로 확정오퍼합니다.)

b) We firmly offer you 100 units of our computer Dreamsys at US$1,000.00 per set CIF New York subject to your reply received within 10 days.
(10일내에 귀사 회신 당사도착 조건부로 당사의 드림시스 컴퓨터 한 대당 1000불 가격으로 100대의 물량을 확정오퍼합니다.)

2) 오퍼 내용이나 거래 조건을 언급한다.

a) For orders of less than 100 pieces at $49 each
For orders of 100-499 pieces at $45 each
Thus for 150 watches the prices will be $6,750. This includes transportation of the watches by air freight.

b)

Item	stock	Quantity	Unit Price	Shipment
Executive Desk	HN31161	2	319.00	March
Total Amount:	US$638.00 CIF Pusan			
Payment:	Draft at sight under an Irrevocable L/C			

c) The time of shipment is within on months after receipt of your credit and the terms of payment is on a draft at 60 d/s under an irrevocable L/C.
(선적 시기는 귀사의 신용장 접수 후 1개월 내로 하고 지급조건은 취소불능신용장에 의거하여 일람 후 60일 출급어음으로 합니다.)

3) 맺음말을 한다.

a) We have enclosed our catalogs with detailed specifications.
(자세한 제품 사양을 포함한 당사의 캐달로그를 동봉합니다.)

b) We hope you will accept this offer without delay.
(귀사가 조속히 이 오퍼를 수용하기를 바랍니다.)

c) We look forward to receiving your order.
(귀사의 주문을 받기를 고대합니다.)

Sample letter

DMS Korea

DMS Korea Co., Inc.
321 Myoung-dong, Chung-ku, Seoul 130-040, Korea
Phone: 02-570-2121/ Fax: 02-570-2122/ Email: Goodnaturekorea@Korea.com

Amherst, Inc.
East 55 Lexington Avenue
Manhattan, New York, NY10050.
phone:(212)556-1234
Fax:(212)556-1235

Dear Sirs,

We offer you firm subject to your acceptance received by Friday, September 30 via DHL under the following terms and conditions:

Item	stock	Quantity	Unit Price	Shipment
Executive Desk	HN31161	2	319.00	March

Total Amount: US$638.00 CIF Pusan
Payment: Draft at sight under an Irrevocable L/C

We look forward very much to receiving your order.

Sincerely,
signature

____

MIN-SHIK CHUNG
Export Manager

13.3 자유오퍼(Free Offer)

유효기간과 선적기일이 명시되지 않으며, 동시에 여러 곳에 오퍼를 진행할 수 있다. 임의적 변경, 취소, 철회가 가능하다.

예) We offer you following goods on the terms and conditions mentioned as below...

13.4 반대오퍼 (Counter Offer)

확정오퍼를 수리하지 않고 자기가 원하는 조건을 제시하는 경우가 있는데, 이를 counter offer라고 한다. 제시된 오퍼의 거래 조건을 그대로 받아들일 수 없을 경우, 그 중 일부나 전체 내용에 대한 수정을 요구하는 오퍼이다. 즉 시일을 앞당기거나 수량을 늘려달라거나, 가격의 인하 등의 내용을 포함하므로 이는 새로운 오퍼로 간주된다. 여러 번의 반대오퍼 과정을 거쳐 한 쪽의 수용(acceptance)이 이루어지게 되고, 이를 기초로 하여 MOU, purchase order form, sales note 등의 방식으로 실질적인 계약이 체결된다.

내용

1) 서신 수취를 확인해 준다.
2) 상대오퍼를 수용할 수 없는 이유를 밝힌다.
3) 맺음말을 한다.

표현연습

1) 서신 수취를 확인해 준다.

a) Thank you for your offer of March 14.
(3월 14일 귀사의 오퍼에 감사드립니다.)

b) We are writing to answer your firm offer of March 14, asking for a price discount.
(가격 할인을 요청하신 3월 14일자 귀사의 확정오퍼에 회신을 드립니다.)

2) 상대오퍼를 수용할 수 없는 이유를 밝힌다.

a) Unfortunately, we cannot grant this request, since the price we quoted is already low.
(유감스럽게도 당사에서 견적을 내드린 가격이 이미 낮으므로 귀사의 요청을 승인할 수 없습니다.)

b) Unfortunately, we are unable to accept a further discount, since the price we quoted is the best we offer.
(유감스럽게도 더 이상의 할인을 받아들일 수 없습니다. 이전에 당사의 견적 가격이 당사가 제공할 수 있는 최선의 가격입니다.)

c) We are very sorry to inform you that it would be difficult to accept your payment terms.
(귀사의 지불조건을 받아들일 수 없음을 통보하게 되어 유감입니다.)

3) 맺음말을 한다.

a) We are looking forward to your prompt reply.
(조속한 회신을 고대합니다.)

b) We hope to have your favorable reply as soon as possible.
(조속한 시일 내에 귀사의 호의적인 회신을 받기를 고대합니다.)

c) We look forward to receiving your acknowledgement of this offer.
(이 오퍼에 대한 수신/접수 확인받기를 고대합니다.)

Sample letter

DMS Korea

DMS Korea Co., Inc.
321 Myoung-dong, Chung-ku, Seoul 130-040, Korea
Phone: 02-570-2121/ Fax: 02-570-2122/ Email: Goodnaturekorea@Korea.com

Amherst, Inc.
East 55 Lexington Avenue
Manhattan, New York, NY10050.
phone:(212)556-1234
Fax:(212)556-1235

Dear Sirs,

We are writing to answer your firm offer of March 14, asking for a price discount.

Unfortunately, we are unable to accept a further discount, since the price we quoted is the best we offer.

We look forward to receiving your acknowledgement of this offer.

Sincerely,
signature

____

MIN-SHIK CHUNG
Export Manager

13.5 조건부오퍼

불확정오퍼의 한 예로 언제든지 내용을 취소나 변경할 수 있는 오퍼이다. 수입업자가 승낙하여도 수출업자의 최종확인 없으면 계약이 성립될 수 없는 오퍼이다. 아래와 같은 문구를 삽입한다.

예)

① 반품허용조건부 오퍼(offer subject to sale or return / offer on sale or return) : 수입업자(피청약자)에게 위탁판매하게 하고 잔여물품을 반납하는 조건으로 서적판매 등에서 주로 이용된다.

This offer is subject to sale or return.

② 점검매매조건부 오퍼(offer on approval) : 오퍼와 함께 물품을 보내어 점검 후 구매의사가 있으면 대금지급, 없으면 반품하는 조건.

③ 최종확인 조건부 오퍼(offer subject to final confirmation / sub-con offer) : 수입업자가 승낙해도 수출업자(청약자)의 최종확인이 있어야 계약이 성립됨. 곧 수입업자의 승낙이 오퍼에 해당한다.

Please note that this offer is subject to our final confirmation.

④ 재고잔류 조건부 오퍼(stock offer / offer subject to being unsold) : 피청약자가 승낙해도 유효재고가 있는 경우에만 계약이 성립된다.

We offer you the above model subject to being unsold.

⑤ 선착순 오퍼(offer subject to prior sale) : 유효재고 범위 내에서 선착순으로 판매하는 것을 조건으로 한다.

⑥ 무확약 오퍼(offer subject to market fluctuation / offer without engagement) : 미확정 가격을 제시하고 시세변동에 따라 예고 없이 가격이 변경될 수 있다.

We offer without engagement.

내용

1) 조건부 오퍼를 밝힌다.

2) 오퍼내용이나 거래 조건을 밝힌다.

3) 맺음말을 한다.

표현연습

1) 조건부 오퍼를 밝힌다.

a) With reference to your quotation of March 30, we take pleasure in offering you without engagement, as follows:
(3월 30일자 귀사의 견적과 관련하여 당사는 아래와 같이 무확약 오퍼를 합니다.)

b) In response to your request of March 9, we are pleased to offer you subject to being unsold as in the following:
(3월 9일자 귀사에 요청에 대한 회신으로 아래와 같이 재고잔류조건부 오퍼를 합니다.)

2) 검토결과를 알려준다.

a) We have studied your quotation and concluded that the amount of US$6,750 is too high.
(귀사의 견적서를 검토한 결과 총 가격이 너무 비싸다는 결론을 내렸습니다.)

b) We carefully reviewed your price list and concluded that the discount rate is a little smaller than we expected.
(귀사의 가격 목록을 검토한 결과 할인율이 기대치보다 적다는 결론을 내렸습니다.)

3) 오퍼내용이나 거래 조건을 밝힌다.

a) Article: Assorted House Slippers
Quantity: 500 pairs
Unit Price: US$20-per pce. (Men's 200; Women's 200; Children's 100)
Amount: US$ 10,000 CIF Inchon
Shipment: During April, subject to seller's receipt of L/C by April 10, 2006

Packing: Pack in plain wooden cases
Payment: By at sight dreaft under L/C

b)

Item	stock	Quantity	Unit Price	Shipment
Executive	Desk HN31161	2	319.00	March
Total Amount: US $638.00 CIF Pusan Payment: Draft at sight under an Irrevocable L/C				

c) We would like you to reduce the price to $1,000. If so, we would be able to order 50 cases.
(가격을 1,000불로 할인해 주시기를 바랍니다. 그러면 50상자를 주문하겠습니다.)

4) 맺음말을 한다.

a) We are looking forward to hearing from you soon.
(조속한 회신을 고대합니다.)

b) We hope to receive your prompt reply by e-mail.
(이메일로 조속한 회신을 고대합니다.)

Sample letter

Amherst, Inc
East 55 Lexington Avenue, Manhattan, New York, NY10050.
phone:(212)556-1234/ Fax:(212)556-1235/ mandmco@finance.com

DMS Korea Co., Inc.
321 Myoung-dong, Chung-ku
Seoul 130-040, Korea
Phone: 02-570-2121
Fax: 02-570-2122

Dear Sirs,

In response to your quotation of March 9, we are sorry to conclude that the amount of US$13,000 is too high. So we have cabled an offer subject to our final confirmation, as follows:

Article: Assorted House Slippers
Quantity: 500 pairs
Unit Price: US$20 per piece. (Men's 200; Women's 200; Children's 100)
Amount: US$10,000 CIF Inchon
Shipment: During April, subject to seller's receipt of L/C by April 10, 2006
Packing: Pack in plain wooden cases
Payment: By at sight draft under L/C

We are sure that you will find this offer to be very reasonable. We are looking forward to hearing from you soon.

Sincerely yours,

signature

____
Don Slobin
Manager

14. 무역 계약(Contract)

14.1 무역계약의 의의:

수출업자와 수입업자가 합의한 내용을 문서화하는 것이기 때문에 꼭 의무적인 것은 아니나, 당사자가 원하는 사항들을 법률적으로 명확히 하여 이행과정에서 생성될 수 있는 문제에 대한 불필요한 분쟁을 미연에 방지할 수 있고, 문제를 조속하고 합리적으로 해결할 수 있게 해준다. 오퍼와 반대오퍼 등 일련의 과정을 거쳐서 상대방의 승낙(acceptance)이 이루어지면 주문과 동시에 신용장을 개설한다.

(참고) 계약서 타이프조항:

상품의 품명, 수량, 선적, 금액, 보험, 지불조건, 화물인, 유효기간 등을 포함한다.

14.2 무역 계약의 종류

- 계약서타이프 조항에 대한 합의가 이루어지면 수출업자가 이러한 조건들이 명시된 Proforma Invoice(견적송장)를 발행하고 수입업자가 이에 대한 별다른 이의를 제기하지 않으면 계약이 체결된 것으로 본다. 하지만 오더의 경우가 크거나 중요한 계약에 한하여 정식으로 계약서를 만들어서 양측이 서명하고 한 부씩 보관한다.

a) 판매 확인서 (Sales note)방식

매도오퍼를 행한 수출업자가 판매확인서 두 통을 작성, 서명하여 수입업자에게 보내면 구입업자는 내용에 이의가 없는 경우 서명하여 한 통은 보관하고 다른 한 통은 돌려보냄으로써 정식 계약서가 성립된다.

b) 구매주문서(Purchase note)방식

정기적으로 대량 구매하는 수입업자는 필요한 상품의 제 조건을 일방적으로 기재, 서명하여 수출업자에게 두 통을 보내면 이를 검토, 이의가 없을 경우 서명하여 한 통은 보관하고 다른 한 통은 다시 수입업자에게 재발송한다.

c) MOU (Memorandum of Understanding: 양해각서)방식

매매 당사자들이 직접 모여서 오퍼를 중심으로 합의된 사항을 계약서로 작성하여

서명, 확인하는 방식으로 가장 일반적으로 이용되며, 특히 플랜트 수출과 같이 거액이면서 내용이 복잡한 경우 효용성이 크다.

d) 개별계약 (Case by Case Contract)

매번 거래가 성립될 때마다 그 거래에 대한 계약서를 작성하고, 오퍼내용을 중심으로 주로 매도인이 작성한다.

e) 포괄 계약(Master Contract)

거래 당사자가 서로 잘 알고 장기간 거래하는 경우, 개별 계약의 번거로움을 피하기 위해 1년 1-2회 포괄계약을 체결하고 이에 의거하여 필요할 때마다 선적해 주는 방식이다.

f) 독점판매계약 (Exclusive Contract)

수출업자는 수입국의 지정수입자 이외에 다른 수입자에게 오퍼하지 않으며, 수입업자는 수출국 다른 업자의 해당 물품을 취급하지 않는 조건으로 이루어지는 계약이다.

14.3 무역 계약의 주요 조건들 (Terms and Conditions)

무역계약을 체결할 때 후일의 오해와 분쟁을 미연에 방지하기 위하여 그 내용을 명확히 하는 동시에 다른 절차나 무역클레임에 대한 해결 방법을 문서화하는 것이 필요하다. 다음은 무역거래에 필수적인 거래 조건 약정들이다.

- 품질조건(quality terms)
- 수량조건(quantity terms)
- 지불조건(payment terms)
- 선적조건(shipment terms)
- 중재조건(arbitration terms)
- 보험조건(insurance terms)
- 포장조건(packing terms)

1) 품질 조건

품질조건에 있어서 품질결정방법, 품질결정시기, 품질증명방법 등의 내용이 규정된다.

1) 품질결정방법 (계약 때)

a. 견본매매 (sale by sample):

가장 보편적인 매매방식으로 신발이나 옷 등 경공업 제품들은 직접 견본을 제시하고 그와 동일 품질을 결정한다.

b. 설명서매매(sale by specification):

기계류, 자동차, 비행기등과 같이 견본을 직접 제시하기 힘든 경우는 설명서, 청사진, 설계도등으로 품질을 결정한다.

c. 상표매매 (sale of trade mark or brand):

Rolex나 Louis Vuitton과 같이 널리 알려진 brand 자체로 품질을 결정한다.

d. 표준품매매 (sale of standard):

농산물, 광산물, 목재 등의 천연산물은 품질의 표준품을 제시해 놓고 이것보다 품질이 우수하면 가격을 높게 책정하고 품질이 나쁘면 할인한다. (F.A.Q. 곡류, 과일; G.M.Q. 목재, 냉동어류; U.S.Q. 원면, 인삼등)

e. 규격매매(sale of grade):

KS, JIS, BSS-12와 같이 상품규격이 국제적으로 규정되어 있거나 공식적 규정으로 규격화된 품질 결정 방법이다.

f. 점검매매(sale of inspection):

매수인이 현품을 직접 확인한 후 체결하는 방식. BWT(Bonded Warehouse Trade: 보세창고거래)

2) 품질 시기 결정방법 (계약 때)

매도인이 선적 시 품질을 보증하느냐, 하역 시 품질을 보증하느냐에 따라 선적품질조건과 하역품질조건으로 나눈다. 일반적으로 FOB, CIF는 선적품질조건을 DEQ (부두인도조건 Delivered Ex. Quay), DDP (관세지급인도조건 Delivered Duty Paid)는 하역품질조건을 따르나 분쟁방지를 위해 계약서에 명기하는 것이 필요하다. 계약 시 당사자 간 협의에 의해 품질 증명이 결정되는데, 통상 선적품질조건에서는 매도인, 하역품질조건에서는 매수인이 품질검사의무의 책임을 진다.

a. 선적 시 품질 (shipped quality)
b. 하역 시 품질 (landed quality)

3) 수량 조건

포장단위 상품이나 개체물품의 경우에는 정확한 개수로 수량을 표시할 있으나, 광물, 곡식과 같은 산물(bulk products)의 경우에는 정확한 수량표현이 불가능하다.

a) 특약에 의한 M/L 조건 (More or Less Clause)

일정한 수량의 과부족 한도를 정해주고 그 범위 내에서 상품을 인도할 경우 계약의 이행으로 보는 조건이다. 특약에 의해 'Quantity shall be subject to variation of 00%'라는 문구를 명시한다.

b) 신용장상 M/L 조항

- 금액, 수량, 단가에 about, circa, approximately 사용 시 10% 이내의 과부족 허용
- 금액, 수량, 단가에 about, circa, approximately 사용 시 5% 이내의 과부족 허용

c) More or Less 조건이 있는 경우 과부족분에 대한 사후 정산이 필요하다. 이때 계약가격, 선적일 가격, 도착일 가격 중 하나를 택하여 매매계약 시 표시해 주는 것이 클레임 예방에 도움이 된다. 표시가 없는 경우는 통상 계약가격을 기준으로 한다.

4) 대금 결제조건

결제 조건은 수출한 물품의 대금을 언제 어떤 방식으로 받아야 하는가에 관한 문제점을 해석 규정하기 위한 조건이다. 결제 조건은 결제 시점과 결제 방식으로 나누어 설명할 수 있다.

- 대금을 결제하는 시기

물품을 받기 전 지급하는 선지급(Payment advance)과, 물건을 구매하면서 지급하는 동시지급(Concurrent payment), 그리고 물품을 받고 나서 지급하는 후지급(Deferred payment)이 있다. 수출업자에게 유리한 선지급을 할 것인가, 아니면 수입업자에게 유리한 후지급을 할 것인가를 정해 서로 효율적인 자금 운영을 해야 한다.

a) 선지급 조건 (Payment advance)

CWO(Cash With Order): 현금 결제방식

상품주문과 동시에 수입업자가 수입대금을 미리 지불함으로써 수출업자되 물품제조를 도모하는 방식으로, 주로 수출업자의 신용이 확실하거나 견본품과 같이 소량을 주문할 때에만 사용된다.

단순 송금방식(remittance base): 송금환 결제방식

주문과 함께 T/T(전신환송금 Telegraphic Transfer)등에 의해 송금하는 방식

b) 동시지급 (Concurrent payment)

COD(현물상환지급 결제방식 Cash on delivery): 현금 결제방식

수출물품이 목적지에 도착하면 수입업자는 직접 상품의 품질을 검사한 후 수입대금을 상품인도와 동시에 현금이 지불되는 방식이다.

CAD(서류인도결제방식 Cash against document): 현금 결제방식

수출업자가 물품을 선적하였음을 입증한 선화증권을 비롯한 선적 서류를 수입업자의 대리점이나 거래은행에 제시하여 서류와 상환으로 현금이 지급되는 방식이다.

D/P(지급인도 결제방식 Documens against payment): 어음 결제방식

무신용장거래에서 어음이 수입업자에게 제시되었을 때 어음대금지급이 있어야 선적서류가 수입업자에게 인도되는 방식이다.

at-sight L/C(일람출급 신용장): 신용장 결제방식

신용장에 의한 거래에서 수출업자 의해 방행된 어음이 수입업자에게 제시되면 수입업자가 이를 일람과 동시에 어음대금을 지급하는 방식이다.

c) 후지급 (외상거래 결제방식 deferred payment)

물품의 선적 또는 인도나 선적서류의 인도가 있은 후 일정한 기간이 경과되어야 대금결제가 이루어지는 외상거래 조건이다. 이러한 지급방식은 수출업자에게는 매우 불리한 조건이다.

D/A (인수인도조건 추심거래 방식 Documents against Acceptance): 어음 결제방식

수입업자의 거래은행이 수입업자에게 운송서류와 함께 환어음을 제시하였을 때 수입업자는 환어음을 인수하나 어음금액은 만기일에 지급하는 외상거래이다.

5) 가격조건을 결정하는 방법 (계약 시)

가격이란 물품거래 시 그 물품의 교환가치를 화폐가치로 표시한 것이므로 수출대금의 결제 등에서 이는 매우 중요하다. 특히 계약시 가격을 도착지조건에 혹은 출발지조건에 따를 것인가를 결정해야 한다. 'INCOTERMS' (International Rules for the Interpretation of Trade Terms) 즉 '무역조건해석에 대한 국제규칙'은 아래와 같은 규정을 통해 무역조건을 통일시키고 있다. INCOTERMS에는 총 11가지 거래조건이 명시되어 있으며 그 중 실무에서 자주 사용되는 세 가지는 다음과 같다.

a. FOB가격 (본선인도가격조건 Free on Board): 화물을 선적하여 항만에 정박하고 있는 본선에 적재까지의 가격을 제시하고 있다.

b. CIF가격 (도착운임 및 보험료포함 가격조건 cost, insurance and freight): FOB가격, 운송비, 보험료를 합친 가격

c. C & F가격 (운임포함 가격조건 cost & freight): FOB가격에 운송비가 가산된 가격

참고) 수출업자의 비용부담 및 임무

	FOB	CFR	CIF
매도인의 비용부담	선적항가지의 비용	FOB비용 목적항까지 운임	FOB비용 및 목적항까지 운임, 보험료
매도인의 임무	수출통관필, 선적완료	수출통관필, 선적완료 해상운송계약체결	수출통관필, 선적완료 해상운송계약체결 해상보험계약체결

참고) 비용(cost)이란?

1) 기본원가 (구입원가와 제조원가)

2) 수출제반비용(포장비, 검사료, 국내운송료, 창고료, 통관료 등)

3) 수출경비 (금리, 통신비, 잡비 등)

6) 선적조건 (계약 시)

선적이란 물품을 모든 운송수단 즉 선박, 비행기, 철도, 택배에 인도하는 것을 뜻하며, 선적조건이란 계약된 물품이 수출업자로부터 수입업자에게 인도되는 시기와 관련되므로 운송 당사자들(수출업자, 수입업자, 선주)은 선적 시기나 방법에 대해 계약을 맺는다.

a) 선적시기

'Shipment is to be made during the first half of August, 2018' (시기 지정)

'The order is to be shipped within 60 days after receipt of L/C. (시기 지정)

'Your goods will be shipped immediately. (시기 미지정)

b) 선적방법

- 분할선적(Partial Shipment): 매매물품이 일정한 경우 전량 선적하지 않고 여러 번 걸쳐 선적하는 것으로 분할선적 여부와 회수 등은 계약서상에 특약되어야 한다.
- 환적(Transshipment): 수출항에서 수입항까지 같은 선박으로 운송되지 않고 도중에 중개항에서 다른 선적으로 재선적하는 것을 의미한다.

'We hope you will consent to our shipping half of the order in September and the other half in October.' (분할선적)

'We cannot ship this order unless you amend the credit to allow transshipments. (환적)

c) 선하증권 (B/L: Bill of Lading)

선하증권은 수출업자가 상선회사와 운송계약을 맺으면 상선회사가 발행하는 일종의 유가증권이다. 상선회사가 위탁받는 물품을 수입항까지 운송하고, 이 선하증권은 신용장 발행은행을 통해 수입업자에게 전달된다. 수입업자는 운송화물을 인도하면서 선하증권을 상선회사에 상환한다.

(참고)

- 선적서류 (Shipping Documents) : 화물 운송 시 수출업자가 수입업자에게 제공하는 서류

  1) 선하증권(B/L, Bill of Lading)

  2) 상업송장(invoice)

  3) 해상보험증권(insurance policy)

  4) 포장명세서(packing list)

  5) 원산지증명서(certificate of origin)

  6) 기타 영사송장, 세관송장, 검사증명서(certificate of inspection) 등

- 선적하인 (shipping marks) : 선적하인은 주로 매수인이 지정해 표시한다.

  1) main mark (주하인)

  2) port mark 혹은 destination mark (항구 혹은 도착지 표시)

  3) case No. (상자번호)

  4) country of origin mark (원산지 표시)

  5) weight (중량)

  6) measurement (용적)

  7) counter mark (부하인: 수출업자나 수입업자가 화물분류상 필요에 따라 하는 표시)

  8) care mark (주의 표시)

예)

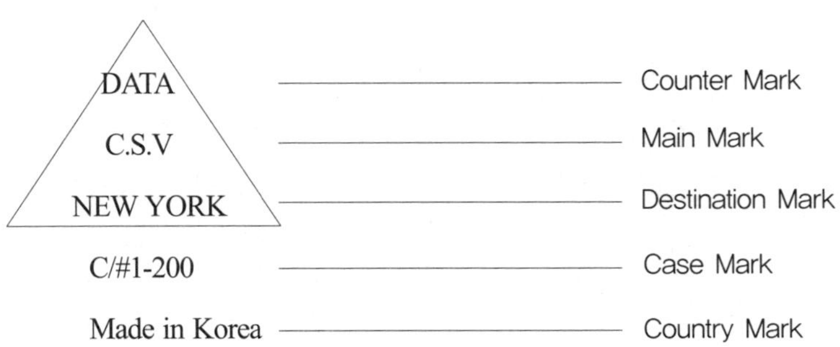

해석) EX outside and C.S.V. in triangle over New York with case numbers one to two hundred and made in Korea

(참고) 주의 표시 (care mark)

Fragile	(깨지기 쉬움)
Guard Against Damp	(습기조심)
Handle with Care	(취급주의)
Keep Cool	(서늘한 곳에 보관)
Keep Dry	(건조한 곳에 보관)
Keep from Heat	(열에 주의)
Keep out of the Sun	(햇빛을 쬐지 말 것)
Hooks	(갈고리 사용금지)
No Upside Down	(거꾸로 들지 말 것)
Perishable Goods	(부패성 식품)
This End Up	(상단)

7) 보험조건 (계약시)

수출업자로부터 수입업자에게 물품이 인도되기까지는 운송과정상에 여러 가지 사고 가능성이 내재한다. 보험자(insurer)인 보험회사는 항해에 관한 사고가 발생했을 경우 피보험자 (insured)에게 그 손해를 보상한다.

반면 무역거래과정에서 해상보험이 포괄할 수 없는 위험인 정치적위험이나 전쟁, 신용상의 위험 등에서 수출업자나 수출자금을 융자한 금융기관의 손해를 보상해 주는 수출진흥을 위한 비영리 정책보험을 수출보험이라 한다.

보험금액은 손해보상범위에 따라 달라질 수 있으나 CIF송장가격에 10%를 더한 것으로 결정된다. 그러므로 해상보험금액은 수입업자의 희망이익(expected profit)를 합쳐 CIF송장가격의 110%로 대하여 보험료를 지불한다. 신용장에 명기되는 다음 표현의 의미를 이해하자.

'Marine Insurance Policy, endorsed in blank, for 110% of the invoice amount Including War Risk' (CIF송장가격 110%에 대한 백지식 배서된 해상보험증권)

(참고)

● 협회적하약관(Institute Cargo Clause)

보험자의 담보위험, 면책보험, 보험기간, 운송약관 등을 포함한다. 현재 구약관과 신약관으로 구분되는데, 구약관과 신약관의 시기구분은 1982년 이전과 이후로 나누어진다. 신협회적하약관은 담보범위를 ICC[A], ICC[B], ICC[C] 세 가지로 구분한다. ICC[A]는 구약관의 A/R (all risks: 전위험담보조건)과 동일하며, ICC[B]는 구약관의 W.A.(with average: 분손담보조건)과 동일하지는 않지만 서로 대응되는 조건이고, ICC[C]는 구약관의 F.P.A.(free from particular average: 단독해손부담보조건)와 대응되는 조건이다. 담보범위의 세목은 다음과 같다. ICC[A]: (1)-(12)/ ICC[B]: (1)-(11)/ ICC[C]: (1)-(7).

● 담보위험 보장내용

(1) fire or explosion (화재나 폭발)

(2) vessel or craft being stranded, grounded, sunk or capsized (선박, 운반선의 좌초, 견인, 침몰, 전복)

(3) overturning or derailment of land conveyance (육상수송용구의 전복, 탈선)

(4) collision or contact of vessel, craft, or conveyance with any external object other than water. (선박, 운반선, 수송용구의 물 이외의 타 물체와 충돌, 접촉)

(5) discharge of cargo at a port of distress (조난항에서의 화물하역작업)

(6) general average sacrifice (공동해손희생 G.A.: 해상운송에서는 선박 및 적하품이 공동의 위험에 직면하였을 경우, 그 손해를 방지하거나 또는 최소한으로 줄이기 위하여 선박 또는 적하품의 일부를 고의로 희생시키거나 비용을 지출하는 일이 있다. 공동해손은 이러한 희생 또는 비용)

(7) jettison (투하: 선박을 구출할 목적으로 적하품의 일부를 투하하는 의미)

(8) earthquake, volcanic eruption or lightning (지진, 화산폭발, 낙뢰)

(9) jettison or washing overboard (투화 혹은 갑판유실)

(10) entry of sea, lake, river water into vessel, craft, hold, conveyance, container, liftvan, or place of storage (본선, 운반선, 선창, 운송용구, 컨테이너, 리프트밴, 본관장소에서의 해수, 호수, 강물의 침입)

(11) total loss of any package lost overboard or dropped whilst loading on to, or unloading from vessel or craft (본선, 운반선에 선적 또는 본선, 우반선에서 화물 중 바다에 떨어지거나 갑판에 추락한 매 포장 당 전체 손실)

(12) all risks of loss of or damage to the subject-matter insured except above (이외에 보험목적에 대한 감실 또한 손상에 대한 위험)

Sample letter

DMS Korea

DMS Korea Co., Inc.
321 Myoung-dong, Chung-ku, Seoul 130-040, Korea
Phone: 02-570-2121/ Fax: 02-570-2122/ Email: Goodnaturekorea@Korea.com

March 30, 2016

AIG General Insurance
3rd floor, Keukdong Bldg
60-1 Chungmu-ro
Chung-ku, Seoul

Dear Sirs:

We shall shortly be making regular shipments of fancy leather goods to South America by approved ships and shall be glad if you will issue an a/r insurance policy for, say, $50,000 to cover these shipments from our warehouse at the above address to port of destination.

All goods will be packed in wooden cases and dispatched by road to Boston and, less frequently, to New York.

Yours faithfully

signature

____

MIN-SHIK CHUNG
Manager

(해석)

당사는 곧 승인된 선편으로 남아메리카에 고급가죽제품을 정기적으로 수송하게 될 것이며, 위 주소에 있는 저희의 창고로부터 도착항까지 적하를 보상받기위한 50,000불의 a/r 증권(all risks(전위험담보조건))을 발행해 주시길 바랍니다. 모든 상품은 나무상자로 포장될 것이며 Boston까지 또 덜 빈번하지만 New York까지는 육로로 수송될 것입니다.

(참고)

일반무역거래협정서 (Agreement on General Terms and Conditions of Business)
수출업자/수입업자들 사이에 계약이 성립되면 장차 있을지 모르는 거래상의 분쟁을 미연에 방지하기 위해 미래 기준안을 마련해 둔다. 주로 거래의 형태, 품질, 가격, 선적, 보험, 결제방법, 오퍼, 주문, 클레임, 중재방법 등을 내용으로 담고 있다. 수출업자가 원본(original)과 부본(duplicate) 2부를 작성하여 수입업자에게 보내면, 수입업자는 이를 검토하고 특별한 이의 사항이 없으면 서명한 다음 그 중 1부를 수출업자에게 발송한다.

일반무역거래 협정서 sample

일반무역거래협정서 (Agreement on General Terms and Conditions of Business)

This agreement entered into between A&B Co., Ltd., Seoul, Korea (hereinafter called Seller) and X&Y Co., Inc., New York, U.S.A (hereinafter called Buyer) witness as follows:

1. Business: Both Seller and Buyer act as Principals and not as Agents.
2. Samples and Quality: Seller is to supply Buyer with samples free of charge, and the quality of the goods to be shipped should be about equal to the sample on which an order is given.
3. Quantity: Weight and Quantity determined by the Seller, as set forth in shipping documents, shall be final.
4. Prices: Unless otherwise specified, prices are to be quoted in U.S. Dollars on CIF New York basis.
5. Firm Offers: All firm offers are to remain effective for three days including the day cabled. Sundays and National Holidays shall not be counted as days.
6. Orders: Except in cases where firm offers are accepted all orders are to be subject to Seller's final confirmation.
7. Packing: Proper export wooden case packing is to be carried out, each case bearing the mark DATA with port mark, running case numbers, and the country of origin.
8. Payment: Drafts shall be to be drawn at 30 d/s under irrevocable Letter of Credit, documents attached, for the full invoice value.

9. Shipment: Shipment is to be made within the time stipulated in each contract, except in circumstances beyond Seller's control. The date of Bill of Lading shall be taken as conclusive proof of the day of shipment.

10. Marine Insurance: All shipments shall be covered on ICC[A] including War Risks. for the invoice amount plus 10 percent. All policies shall be made out in U.S. Dollar and claims payable in New York.

11. Force Majeure: Seller shall not be responsible for the delay in shipment due to force majeure, including fires, earthquakes, tempest, strikes, lockouts, mobilization, war, prohibition of export, and any other contingencies which may prevent shipment within the period stipulated. In the event of any of the aforesaid causes arising, documents proving its occurrence or existence shall be sent by Seller to Buyer without delay.

12. Delayed Shipment: In all cases of force majeure provided in the Article No. 10 the period should still be prevented by a continuance of the causes mentioned in the Article No. 10 or the consequences of any of them, it shall be at Buyer's option either to allow the shipment of late goods or to cancel the order by giving Seller the notice of cancellation by cable.

13. Claims: Claims, if any, shall be submitted by cable within fourteen (14) days after arrival of goods at destination. Certificates by recognized surveyors shall be sent by mail without delay.

14. Arbitration: All claims which cannot be amicably settled by arbitration in Seoul, Korea, in accordance with the Commercial Arbitration Rules of the Korea Commercial Arbitration Board.

This Agreement shall be valid on and after March 20, 2006.

(Buyer) X&Y Co., Inc.	(Seller) A&B Co., Ltd.
(Signed)	(Signed)

(해석)

대한민국 서울 A&B주식회사(이하 매도인이라 칭함)와 미국 뉴욕의 X&Y상사(이하 매수인이라 칭함) 사이에 체결된 이 협정서는 아래 의 것들을 입증한다.

1. 거래방식: 거래는 매도인과 매수인이 대행사이 아닌 주체로 행해져야 한다.
2. 견본품과 품질: 매도인은 매수인에게 무료로 견본을 제공하며, 출하된 상품의 품질은 주문 시와 동일해야 한다.
3. 수량: 선적서류에도 제시되었듯이 매도인이 결정한 무게와 수량이 최종적이다.
4. 가격: 별도의 명시된 바가 없는 한, 가격은 미국달러화 표시 뉴욕도착 운임 및 보험료포함가격으로 견적된다.
5. 확정오퍼: 모든 확정오퍼는 전송된 날짜를 포함해 3일 동안 유효하다. 일요일과 국경일은 제외된다.
6. 주문: 확정오퍼가 받아들여진 경우를 제외하고는 매도인의 최종 확인을 조건으로 한다.
7. 포장: 적절한 수출용 목재상자 포장이 행해져야 하며, 각 상자에는 항구표시, 일렬상자번호, 원산지표시를 포함한 DATA화인이 있어야 한다.
8. 결제: 취소불능신용장에 의거하여 운송서류를 첨부하여 송장총액에 대해 일람 후 30일 출금 환어음을 발행한다.
9. 선적: 선적은 매도인의 불가항력의 상황을 제외하고는 각 계약서에 명시된 기간 내에 해야 한다. 선하증권의 발행일자는 선적일의 결정적인 증거로 간주된다.
10. 해상보험: 모든 적하품은 송장금액에 10%를 더한 110%의 금액을 전쟁위험 포함한 ICC[A]조건으로 부보한다. 모든 보험증권은 미국 달러화로, 보험금은 뉴욕에서 지급되는 것으로 작성한다.
11. 불가항력: 매도인은 불가항력에 기인하여 발생한 선적지연에 대해서는 책임을 지지 않는다. 불가항력이란 정해진 선적기일의 선적을 방해하는 화재, 홍수, 지진, 태풍, 동맹파업, 공장폐쇄, 동원, 전쟁, 수출금지 및 기타 우발사고를 말한다. 전술한 원인이 발생한 경우에는 그 발생 및 존재를 증명하는 서류를 지체 없이 매도인이 매수인에게 제시해야 한다.
12. 선적지연: 제 10항에 규정되어 있는 모든 불가항력의 경우에 있어서 정해진 선적기간은 21일간 연기되어야 한다. 이와 같이 연기된 기일 내에 선적이 제 10항에 명시되어 있는 원인의 존속 혹은 그 결과 때문에 방해받고 있는 경우에는 매수인은 지적된 상품의 선적을 허용하느냐를 전신으로 주문취소의 통지를 매도인에게 보냄으로써 주문을 취소하느냐하는 선택권을 가진다.
13. 클레임: 만약 클레임이 발생하면 목적지항에 상품이 도착한 후 14일 이내에 제기해야 한다. 공인검사인의 증명서가 지체 없이 우편으로 송부되어야 한다.
14. 중재: 매도인과 매수인 사이에 원만하게 해결이 되는 않는 클레임은 대한상사중재원의 규칙에 의거해 한국, 서울시에서 중재에 의해 해결되어야 한다.

이 협정서는 2006년 3월 20일부터 유효할 것이다.

(참고) 무역클레임 (claim)

무역 계약을 할 때 수출업자나 수업업자가 계약을 이행하지 않고, 그로 인하여 손해를 입은 당사자가 권리를 회복, 손해배상, 계약의 파기 등을 주장하는 권리를 말한다. 무역클레임은 일반적으로 무역거래상의 클레임을 의미하며, 운송 중의 사고나 손상된 화물에 대한 배상 요구도 포함한다.

15. 승낙(Acceptance)

반대 오퍼(counter offer)를 몇 번 반복하면서 합의에 이르게 되고, 한 쪽에서 오퍼를 승낙함으로써 무역 계약이 체결된다.

내용

1) 서신 수취를 확인한다.
2) 상대 의사를 조건부로 수용한다.
3) 맺음말을 한다.

표현연습

1) 서신 수취를 확인한다.

a) Thank you for your letter of March 30, 2017, asking for a lower price.
(낮은 가격을 요청하신 2017년 3월 30일자 서신에 감사드립니다.)

b) I appreciate your letter asking for an extra 5% discount.
(5% 추가할인을 요청하신 서신에 감사드립니다.

2) 상대 의사를 조건부로 수용한다.

a) We are accepting your request on this particular order. The maximum we can grant is 15%.
(특별 주문에 대해 귀사의 요청을 수락합니다. 당사 허용할 수 있는 최대치는 15%이다.)

b) If you place your order with us by the end of this month, we will accept your request.
(이번 달 말까지 주문을 하신다면, 당사는 귀사의 요청을 수락하겠습니다.)

c) If you place an order for more than 10 dozens, we will give your a 3% discount.
(120대 이상 주문 시 3%의 할인을 제공하겠습니다.)

d) We could give you a 10% discount on the condition that you order more than 1,000 pieces.
(1000이상 주문을 조건으로 10%할인을 제공합니다.)

3) 맺음말을 한다.

a) I hope these conditions are acceptable and look forward to hearing from you.
(이 조건들이 수용가능하기를 바라며, 회신을 고대합니다.)

b) I look forward to your prompt reply.
(조속한 회신을 고대합니다.)

Sample letter 1

DMS Korea

DMS Korea Co., Inc.
321 Myoung-dong, Chung-ku, Seoul 130-040, Korea
Phone: 02-570-2121/ Fax: 02-570-2122/ Email: Goodnaturekorea@Korea.com

Amherst, Inc.
East 55 Lexington Avenue
Manhattan, New York, NY10050.
phone:(212)556-1234
Fax:(212)556-1235

Dear Sirs,

Thank you for your fax of March 14 asking for an extra 5% on the discount.

If you place your order with us by the end of this month, we will accept this request. I hope this will be acceptable.

Looking forward to hearing from you soon.

Sincerely,
signature

____

MIN-SHIK CHUNG
Export Manager

Sample letter 2

DMS Korea

DMS Korea Co., Inc.

321 Myoung-dong, Chung-ku, Seoul 130-040, Korea

Phone: 02-570-2121/ Fax: 02-570-2122/ Email: Goodnaturekorea@Korea.com

Amherst, Inc.
East 55 Lexington Avenue
Manhattan, New York, NY10050.
phone:(212)556-1234
Fax:(212)556-1235

Dear Sirs,

Thank you for your letter of March 14 asking for a lower price.

We are accepting your request on this particular order. I hope that this condition is acceptable.

We are looking forward to hearing from you soon.

Sincerely,
signature

____

MIN-SHIK CHUNG
Export Manager

16. 계약서의 커버레터

내용

1) 계약서 동봉을 알린다.

2) 상대방에게 계약내용 재확인 요청을 한다.

3) 서명 후 계약서 한 부를 반송할 것을 언급한다.

4) 맺음말을 한다.

표현연습

1) 계약서 동봉을 알린다.

a) We have enclosed one copy(a draft) of the agreement.

2) 상대방에게 계약내용 재확인 요청을 한다.

a) Would you please check these documents and confirm that there are no misunderstanding or errors?
(서류를 검토하시고 오해나 오식이 없는지를 확인해 주세요.)

b) Would you please review the contents and make sure that there are no errors and omissions?
(내용을 검토하시고 오식이나 누락된 것이 없는지 확인해 주세요.)

3) 서명 후 계약서 한 부를 반송할 것을 언급한다.

a) Please sign both sets and return on set to us with your signature.
(2부 서명하고 1부를 당사로 보내주세요.)

b) Please initial and send back to us.
(가서명해 당사로 보내주세요.)

4) 맺음말을 한다.

a) If you have any comments, please let us know as soon as you can.
(의견이 있으면 조속히 연락주세요.)

b) If there are any discrepancies in the agreement, please inform us as soon as possible.
(계약서에 일치하지 않는 사항이 있다면 조속히 알려주세요.)

Sample letter 1

DMS Korea

DMS Korea Co., Inc.
321 Myoung-dong, Chung-ku, Seoul 130-040, Korea
Phone: 02-570-2121/ Fax: 02-570-2122/ Email: Goodnaturekorea@Korea.com

Amherst, Inc.
East 55 Lexington Avenue
Manhattan, New York, NY10050.
phone:(212)556-1234
Fax:(212)556-1235

Dear Sirs,

We have enclosed a draft of the agreement which was approved at the March 14 meeting.

Would you please review and confirm that there are errors and omissions? Then initial and send back to us. Also, if you have any comments, please let us know.

We will prepare a formal agreement by April 10 and mail two copies to you for signature.

Sincerely,
signature

____

MIN-SHIK CHUNG
Export Manager

Sample letter 2

DMS Korea

DMS Korea Co., Inc.
321 Myoung-dong, Chung-ku, Seoul 130-040, Korea
Phone: 02-570-2121/ Fax: 02-570-2122/ Email: Goodnaturekorea@Korea.com

Amherst, Inc.
East 55 Lexington Avenue
Manhattan, New York, NY10050.
phone:(212)556-1234
Fax:(212)556-1235

Dear Sirs,

We sent three copies of the Sales Agreement for review and signature two weeks ago, but have not heard from you.

Would you please let me know what the status is right away? We need two signed copies before placing an order.

We look forward to hearing from you soon.

Sincerely,
signature

____

MIN-SHIK CHUNG
Export Manager

17. 주문서의 커버레터

내용

1) 서신 수취를 확인하고, 주문 상품을 언급한다.

2) 동봉물과 지불 방법을 언급한다.

3) 선적일을 언급한다

표현연습

1) 서신 수취를 확인하고, 주문 상품을 언급한다.

a) We would like to order two Model 5000 engines.
(모델 5000형 엔진 두개를 주문합니다.)

b) Thank you for your quotation for 30 pieces of the No. 55 part.
(부품 55번 30개에 대한 견적에 감사드립니다.)

2) 동봉물과 지불 방법을 언급한다.

a) We have enclosed Purchase Order (No. 333) and a check of $5,000.
(333번 구매주문서와 5,000불짜리 수표를 동봉합니다.)

b) Would you please charge to the following card:
(아래 카드번호로 결제를 청구합니다.)

Name: David Lamb

VISA Card: Card Number 456-3342-5666

Valid until August 2017

3) 선적일을 언급한다.

a) Would you please sent it to us as soon as you can?
(가능한 빨리 물품을 보내주세요.)

b) Would you please make shipment immediately?
(즉시 선적해 주세요.)

c) Would you please assure us that they will reach us by March 20 at the latest?
(늦어도 3월 20일까지 확실히 당사에 도착할 수 있도록 조처해 주세요.)

d) Would you please send us the shipping schedule?
(출하일정을 당사로 보내주세요.)

e) Would you please inform us of the expected shipping date?
(선적 예정일을 당사로 보내주세요.)

Sample letter 1

Amherst, Inc
East 55 Lexington Avenue, Manhattan, New York, NY10050
phone:(212)556-1234/ Fax:(212)556-1235/ mandmco@finance.com

DMS Korea Co., Inc.
321 Myoung-dong, Chung-ku
Seoul 130-040, Korea
Phone: 02-570-2121
Fax: 02-570-2122

Dear Sirs,

Woodside Tea Cup (Model No. 345)

Thank you very much for your quotation of March 22 for 150 Woodside Tea Cups (Model No. 345).

The discount on orders of over 100 pieces makes the price satisfactory and so we are enclosing our Order (No. 745) together with a banker's draft for $6,750 as requested.

Would you please let me know the delivery date?

Best regards,

signature

DAN SLOBIN
Manager

Sample letter 2

Amherst, Inc
East 55 Lexington Avenue, Manhattan, New York, NY10050
phone:(212)556-1234/ Fax:(212)556-1235/ mandmco@finance.com

DMS Korea Co., Inc.
321 Myoung-dong, Chung-ku
Seoul 130-040, Korea
Phone: 02-570-2121
Fax: 02-570-2122

Dear Sirs,

We would like to purchase Woodside Tea Cup (Model No. 345).

If you accept payment by credit card, please charge as follows:

Name: DAN SLOBIN
VISA Card: Card Number 456-3342-5666-3672
Valid until August 2010

Would you please inform us of the shipping date?

Best regards,

signature

____

DAN SLOBIN
Manager

18. 주문품 발송 통지

내용

1) 서신 수취를 확인한다.
2) 송장과 출하방법을 통보한다.
3) 동봉한 발송통지서에 서명 후 한 부 반송 요청한다.

표현연습

1) 서신 수취를 확인한다.

a) Thank you very much for your order of March 24.
(3월 24일자 귀사 주문에 감사드립니다.)

b) Thank you for your payment of $50,000 made on March 24.
(3월 24일자 귀사의 50,000불 지불에 감사드립니다.)

c) Thank you for your Order No. 334 and the banker's draft for $6,750.
(334호 주문과 6750불짜리 은행어음에 감사드립니다.)

2) 송장과 출하방법을 통보한다.

a) We are sending our delivery notice along with the signed duplicate of the order form as an acknowledge of the order.
(귀사에 발송통지서와 주문 확인을 위한 주문서 사본을 보내드립니다.)

b) We are sending our invoice and also a receipt of $6,750 to you.
(귀사에 송장과 6750불 영수증을 보내드립니다.)

c) We have shipped the product to you as follows:
(물품을 아래와 같이 출하합니다.)

Shipping Date: (출하일)
Shipping Agent: (선박회사)
Port of Arrival: (도착항)
Carrier: (선박명)

Contents: (선적 내용)
Others: (기타)

d) We shipped your order via DHL on March 24, and you should receive it within five to seven days.

3) 동봉한 발송통지서에 서명 후 한 부 반송 요청한다.

a) Would you please sign the enclosed delivery notice and return it to us by fax?
(동봉한 발송통지서에 서명하여 팩스로 송부해 주십시오.)

b) Would you please confirm receipt of our invoice?
(당사의 송장 수취를 확인해 주세요.)

c) Would you please check that all the contents are included, then sign the enclosed notice and return a copy to us?
(주문의 내용을 확인하고 동봉된 발송통지서에 서명해서 당사로 보내주세요.)

Sample letter 1

DMS Korea

DMS Korea Co., Inc.
321 Myoung-dong, Chung-ku, Seoul 130-040, Korea
Phone: 02-570-2121/ Fax: 02-570-2122/ Email: Goodnaturekorea@Korea.com

Amherst, Inc.
East 55 Lexington Avenue
Manhattan, New York, NY10050.
phone:(212)556-1234
Fax:(212)556-1235

Dear Sirs,

Thank you very much for your order of March 24 (No. 334).

We are sending our delivery notice and the product to you as follows:
Shipping Date: March 30, 2017
Port of Arrival: New York
Carrier: Daehanho 21

Would you please check that all contents are included, then sign the enclosed notice and return a copy to our company?

Sincerely,

signature

____

MIN-SHIK CHUNG
Export Manager

Sample letter 2

DMS Korea

DMS Korea Co., Inc.
321 Myoung-dong, Chung-ku, Seoul 130-040, Korea
Phone: 02-570-2121/ Fax: 02-570-2122/ Email: Goodnaturekorea@Korea.com

Amherst, Inc.
East 55 Lexington Avenue
Manhattan, New York, NY10050.
phone:(212)556-1234
Fax:(212)556-1235

Dear Sirs,

Thank you for your order No. 745 and the banker's draft for $6590. As requested, we are enclosing the signed duplicate of the order form as acknowledgement of the order, and a receipt for $ 6590.

The Woodside Tea Cups (Model No. 345) will be delivered the day after tomorrow and then you should receive them within 5 to 7 days.

We look forward to doing further business with you.

Sincerely,

signature

____

MIN-SHIK CHUNG
Export Manager

Writing Practice

3월 24일 귀사의 주문에 감사드립니다. 당사는 주문품을 3월 30일에 DHL로 보냈고, 7일 이내로 그 물품을 받으실 수 있을 것입니다. 운송 후 물품에 손상이 있는지, 또 모든 내용물들이 포함되어 있는지를 확인해주세요. 문제나 의문이 있을시 당사로 연락 바랍니다.

19. 주문품 독촉

내용

1) 주문한 날짜를 밝히고, 주문품의 미도착을 알린다.

2) 출하정보를 의뢰한다.

3) 사후조처를 언급한다.

표현연습

1) 주문한 날짜를 밝히고, 주문품의 미도착을 알린다.

a) We ordered the product from you on March 12. However, we have not received it as of March 24.
(당사는 3월 12일에 귀사에 제품을 주문했으나 3월 24일 현재 받지 못했습니다.)

b) We sent a purchase order (No. 745) to you on March 24. Unfortunately, it has not yet reached us.
(당사는 3월 24일에 귀사로 구매주문서를 보냈습니다. 유감스럽게도 아직 제품이 미도착했습니다.)

c) One month has passed since you confirmed receipt of our purchase order and the shipping date, but we have not received it yet.
(귀사가 구매주문서 수취와 선적일을 확인한 이래 한달이 지났으나 아직 물품을 수취하지 못했습니다.)

2) 출하정보를 의뢰한다.

a) Please send the shipping information as soon as possible.
(조속히 출하정보를 보내 주십시오.)

b) Would you please check with your shipping section and let us know the status?
(출하부서와 의논하여 현재 상황을 알려주십시오.)

c) Would you please check on the status of the shipment as soon as you can?
(조속히 출하상황을 검토해 주십시오.)

3) 사후조처를 언급한다.

a) We have enclosed a copy of our purchase order (No. 745).
(구매주문서 한부를 동봉합니다.)

b) We will have to cancel the order if it does not arrive by March 30.
(3월 30일까지 미도착시 주문을 취하하겠습니다.)

c) We might otherwise reconsider future orders.
(그렇지 않으면 앞으로의 주문을 재고하겠습니다.)

Sample letter

Amherst, Inc

East 55 Lexington Avenue, Manhattan, New York, NY10050

phone:(212)556-1234/ Fax:(212)556-1235/ mandmco@finance.com

DMS Korea Co., Inc.
321 Myoung-dong, Chung-ku
Seoul 130-040, Korea
Phone: 02-570-2121
Fax: 02-570-2122

Dear Sirs,

We ordered Model No. 334 from you on March 24, 2017. However, it has not reached us yet.

Would you please check with your shipping section and let us know the status as soon as possible?

We will reconsider future orders if it does not arrive by March 30.

Best regards,

signature

DAN SLOBIN
Manager

Writing Practice

2017년 3월 24일에 33형 모델 3대를 위한 구매주문서(745호)를 보냈습니다. 귀사는 주문의 수령과 4월 20일 출하일을 확인했습니다. 그러나 물품이 아직 도착하지 않았습니다. 조속히 출하상황을 점검해 주십시오, 당사의 구매주문서(745호)를 1부 동봉합니다.

20. 출하지연 독촉

내용

1) 출하지연 서신 수취를 확인해 준다.
2) 출하지연을 수용할 경우의 표현
3) 출하지연을 거절할 경우의 표현
4) 출하지연 독촉과 함께 주문 내용을 수정할 경우의 표현

표현연습

1) 출하지연 서신 수취를 확인해 준다.

a) Thank you very much for informing me that the product is not available until March 30.
(3월 30일까지 재고품이 없음을 알려주셔서 감사합니다.)

b) We appreciate your informing us that the price of the product has been changed.
(물품의 가격 변경을 알려주셔서 감사합니다.)

c) Thank you for letting us know that the shipment will be delayed.
(출하 지연을 통보해 주셔서 감사합니다.)

2) 출하지연을 수용할 경우의 표현

a) The shipping delay is acceptable to us. Would you please ship it to us as soon as you can?
(출하지연을 수용하겠습니다. 조속히 주문품을 출하해 주십시오.)

b) Would you please send it to us as soon as it is manufactured?
(제조되는 대로 조속히 보내 주십시오.)

c) We would like to wait until March 30.
(3월 30일까지 기다리겠습니다.)

3) 출하지연을 거절할 경우의 표현

a) Since we must deliver the product to our customer by March 30, the delay in shipment is not acceptable.
(3월 30일까지 당사 고객에게 납품해야 하므로 출하지연을 수용할 수 없습니다.)

b) Since the budget is limited, the price change is not acceptable.
(예산의 제한으로 가격변동을 수용할 수 없습니다.)

c) Please cancel our order and send the confirmation sheet of cancellation.
(당사의 주문을 취하하고 확인증을 보내주십시오.)

d) Would you please ship it by March 30? If not, we will have to cancel this order.
(3월 30일까지 선적해 주십시오. 불가능하다면 이 주문을 취하하겠습니다.)

e) Please cancel our order and refund the money.
(당사의 주문을 취하하고 대금을 환불해 주십시오.)

4) 출하지연 독촉과 함께 주문 내용을 수정할 경우의 표현

a) We would like to order another product.
(다른 제품을 주문하겠습니다.)

b) Please send us a sample or your latest product catalog.)
(당사로 견본 혹은 귀사의 최근 제품 캐달로그를 보내주십시오.)

c) Please replace the product with another one, Model No. 335.
(그 제품을 다른 335번 모델로 대체해 주십시오.)

d) We would like to order Model No. 335, instead. Please ship it as soon as possible.
(대신 335번 모델을 주문하겠습니다. 가능한 조속히 그것을 출하해주십시오.)

Sample letter

Amherst, Inc
East 55 Lexington Avenue, Manhattan, New York, NY10050
phone:(212)556-1234/ Fax:(212)556-1235/ mandmco@finance.com

DMS Korea Co., Inc.
321 Myoung-dong, Chung-ku
Seoul 130-040, Korea
Phone: 02-570-2121
Fax: 02-570-2122

Dear Sirs,

We thank you for letting us know that Model No. 335 is not available until March 30, 2017.

A delay in shipment of two weeks is acceptable, but we must be able to deliver the order to our customer by April 30. Would you please ship it by March 30? If not, we will have to cancel this order.

Please confirm. We are looking forward to receiving your reply by March 20.

Sincerely,

signature

____

DAN SLOBIN
Manager

Writing Practice

335번 모델 프린터의 재고가 없어 2017년 3월 30일까지 선적이 지연됨을 알려주셔서 감사합니다. 당사는 3월 30일까지는 기다리겠습니다. 그때까지 선적이 불가능하다면 다른 제품을 주문하겠습니다. 당사로 캐달로그를 보내주십시오.

21. 상품훼손 및 수량부족 항의 서신

내용

1) 제품 수취를 확인한다.
2) 문제점을 통보한다.
3) 문제 해결책을 제시한다.
4) 맺음말을 한다.

표현연습

1) 제품 수취를 확인한다.

a) We received the product from you on March 30.
(3월 30일에 귀사 제품을 수취했습니다.)

2) 문제점을 통보한다.

a) However, the quantity was not correct.
(그런데 수량이 정확하지 않습니다.)

b) Only five instead of ten units were delivered. 5 units were missing.
(10대중 오직 5대만이 배송되었습니다. 5대가 부족합니다.)

c) They were different from the sample.
(견본과 품질이 상이합니다.)

d) 5 units out of 10 were damaged.
(10대중 5대가 손상되었습니다.)

e) The actual quantity did not match the invoice quantity.
(실제 수량이 송장에 첨부된 수량과 일치하지 않습니다.)

3) 문제 해결책을 제시한다.

a) Would you please this order and let us know the results as soon as you can?
(주문을 검토하시고 조속히 결과를 알려주십시오.)

b) Would you please send the product with the correct color to us by March 24?
(3월 24일까지 정확한 색상의 제품을 보내주십시오.)

c) Would you please send the remaining sets to us?
(잔여분을 보내 주십시오.)

d) Please accept cancellation of this order.
(이 주문의 취하를 수락해 주십시오.)

e) We would like to cancel this order. Please let us know whether you can accept it or not.
(이 주문을 취하하겠습니다. 취하를 수락하실 수 있는지를 알려주십시오.)

f) We would like to return the product to you for replacement. Would this be acceptable to you?
(교환을 위해 제품을 반송하겠습니다. 귀사가 이것을 수락하여 주실 수 있는지요?

4) 맺음말을 한다.

a) Please let us know the expected shipping date by fax.
(출하예정일을 팩스로 통보해 주십시오.)

b) Would you please do your best to avoid this kind of problem in the future?
(앞으로 이런 종류의 문제가 발생하지 않도록 최선을 다해 주십시오.)

c) Would you please make sure that this kind of problem does not happen in the future?
(앞으로 이런 문제가 발생하지 않도록 해 주십시오.)

Sample letter

Amherst, Inc
East 55 Lexington Avenue, Manhattan, New York, NY10050
phone:(212)556-1234/ Fax:(212)556-1235/ mandmco@finance.com

DMS Korea Co., Inc.
321 Myoung-dong, Chung-ku
Seoul 130-040, Korea
Phone: 02-570-2121
Fax: 02-570-2122

Dear Sirs,

We received 200 pieces of Model No. 244 from you on March 24.

However, the color was different from the sample color in your catalog. We would like to return it to you for replacement. Would this be acceptable to you?

We are looking forward to hearing from you soon.

Sincerely,

signature

DAN SLOBIN
Manager

Writing Practice

3월 24일 귀사로부터 224번 모델 2세트를 수취했습니다. 그러나 이번 당사는 구매주문서(745호)에 의거해 4세트를 주문했습니다. 조속히 잔여분 2세트를 출하해 주십시오. 출하예정을 팩스로 통보해 주십시오.

22. 상품훼손 및 수량부족 항의서신 회신

내용

1) 항의 서신 수취를 확인한다.
2) 문제 해결책을 제시한다.
3) 맺음말을 한다.

표현연습

1) 항의 서신 수취를 확인한다.

a) Thank you very much for writing us about the product you have recently purchased.
(최근 구매하신 제품에 대한 귀사의 서신에 감사드립니다.)

b) Thank you form informing us of the wrong shipment.
(잘못된 출하를 통보해 주셔서 감사합니다.)

2) 문제 해결책을 제시한다.

a) We will ship the missing products to you right away.
(즉시 부족분을 귀사로 배송하겠습니다.)

b) We will send a corrected invoice to you promptly.
(즉시 정정된 송장을 귀사에 보내드리겠습니다.)

c) We will ship a replacement to you promptly. In the meantime, would you please return the incorrect product to us?
(즉시 대체품을 보내드리겠습니다. 그런데 잘못된 제품을 반송해 주시겠습니까?)

d) Would you please return the defective product to us for examination?
(검사를 위해 손상된 제품을 당사로 반송해 주시겠습니까?)

3) 맺음말을 한다.

a) We will inform you of the results as soon as possible.
(가능하면 빨리 결과를 통보해 드리겠습니다.)

Sample letter

DMS Korea

DMS Korea Co., Inc.
321 Myoung-dong, Chung-ku, Seoul 130-040, Korea
Phone: 02-570-2121/ Fax: 02-570-2122/ Email: Goodnaturekorea@Korea.com

Amherst, Inc.
East 55 Lexington Avenue
Manhattan, New York, NY10050.
phone:(212)556-1234
Fax:(212)556-1235

Dear Sirs,

Thank you for your letter of March 24, informing us of the damage to the Model 224 display that we shipped to you on March 10.

Would you please return the unit to us so that we can examine the cause of the problem?

In the meantime, we will send a replacement unit to you by the end of this week.

Sincerely,

signature

____

MIN-SHIK CHUNG
Export Manager

Writing Practice

모델 224번의 훼손을 통보해 주셔서 감사드립니다. 검사를 위해 손상된 제품을 당사로 반송해 주시겠습니까? 즉시 대체품을 보내드리겠습니다.

23. 대금지급 통지

내용

1) 수입업자는 대금청구서 수취를 통보한다.

2) 대금지불 방법을 알린다.

3) 수령증 송달을 요청한다.

표현연습

1) 수입업자는 대금청구서 수취를 통보한다.

a) Thank you for your invoice dated March 24.
(3월 24일자 귀사의 송장(대금청구서)에 감사드립니다.

b) Thank you for your letter asking for payment on our order (No. 223).
(주문 223호에 대한 지불을 요청하신 귀사의 서신을 수취했습니다.)

2) 대금지불 방법을 알린다.

a) We are sending you a check for $50,000 on my order No. 223.
(주문서 223호에 대해 50,000불을 수표로 보내드립니다.)

b) We are sending you $50,000 on my order No. 223 by Bill of Exchange.
(주문서 223호에 대해 50,000불을 환어음으로 보내드립니다.)

c) We are wiring $50,000 to your bank on my order No. 223.
(주문서 223호에 대해 50,000불을 귀사 거래은행으로 전송합니다.)

d) We have remitted $50,000 to your bank account on our order No. 223.
(주문서 223호에 대해 50,000불을 귀사의 은행계좌로 송금했습니다.)

e) We will pay the balance within two months.
(두 달 내로 잔금을 지불하겠습니다.)

3) 수령증 송달을 요청한다.

a) Would you please send us confirmation of receipt by fax?
(수령확인증을 팩스로 보내 주세요.)

b) Please confirm that the payment has been made.
(대금 지금을 확인해 주십시오.)

Sample letter

Amherst, Inc
East 55 Lexington Avenue, Manhattan, New York, NY10050
phone:(212)556-1234/ Fax:(212)556-1235/ mandmco@finance.com

DMS Korea Co., Inc.
321 Myoung-dong, Chung-ku
Seoul 130-040, Korea
Phone: 02-570-2121
Fax: 02-570-2122

Dear Sirs,

Thank you for your letter of March 24, requesting payment of the balance of $50,000 on INVOICE NO. 245.

We are sending this amount to you on my order No. 223 by check. Would you please send us confirmation of receipt by fax.

Thank you for your business.

Sincerely,

signature

____

DAN SLOBIN
Manager

Writing Practice

3월 30일자 귀사의 대금 청구서를 수취했습니다. 주문 223호에 대해 50,000불을 귀사의 은행계좌로 송금했습니다. 회신으로 (by return) 완불에 대한 영수증을 보내주십시오.

24. 대금수령 확인 통지

내용

1) 대금 수취를 알린다.

2) 지속적이고 우호적인 유대 관계를 언급한다.

표현연습

1) 대금 수취를 알린다.

a) Thank you for your payment of $50,000 on our invoice No. 223 of March 24.
(3월 24일자 송장번호 223호에 근거해 50,000불을 지불해 주셔서 감사드립니다.)

b) We confirm today your payment on our invoice (No. 223).
(송장번호 223호에 근거한 귀사의 지불을 금일 확인했습니다.)

c) We have received your check for $50,000 on our invoice of March 24 (No. 223).
(3월 24일자 송장번호 223호에 근거해 50,000불짜리 수표를 수취했습니다.)

2) 지속적이고 우호적인 유대 관계를 언급한다.

a) We hope that our products will meet your expectations and look forward to hearing from you again.
(당사 제품에 대한 만족을 기원하며 회신을 고대합니다.)

b) Hopefully our products meet your expectations and look forward to the possibility of doing business with you again.
(당사 제품에 대한 만족을 기원하며 귀사와 새로운 거래가 가능하기를 고대합니다.)

c) We are confident that our products are entirely satisfactory and welcome you comments.
(당사 제품에 틀림없이 만족하리라 믿으며 귀사의 의견을 환영합니다.)

Sample letter

DMS Korea

DMS Korea Co., Inc.
321 Myoung-dong, Chung-ku, Seoul 130-040, Korea
Phone: 02-570-2121/ Fax: 02-570-2122/ Email: Goodnaturekorea@Korea.com

Amherst, Inc.
East 55 Lexington Avenue
Manhattan, New York, NY10050.
phone:(212)556-1234
Fax:(212)556-1235

Dear Sirs,

As of March 24, we confirmed your payment on our invoice (No. 223).

We hope that our products meet your expectations and look forward to the possibility of doing business with you again.

If there are any questions about our products, Please let us know.

Sincerely,

signature

MIN-SHIK CHUNG
Export Manager

Writing Practice

3월 24일자 송장번호 223호에 근거한 50,000불을 지불해 주셔서 감사드립니다. 당사 제품에 대해 만족하시기를 기대하며, 앞으로 지속적인 거래를 고대합니다. 질문 사항이 있으면 부담 없이 연락주세요.

25. 지불 독촉

내용

1) 지불 지체를 통보한다.

2) 지불 독촉과 관련될 서류를 동봉함을 알린다.

표현연습

1) 지불 지체를 통보한다.

a) Unfortunately, we have not yet received payment on our invoice No. 223.
(유감스럽게도 송장번호 223호에 근거한 지불을 아직 수취하지 못했습니다.)

b) Regretfully, we remind you that the amount for your March 24 order is overdue.
(유감스럽게도 3월 24일 귀사의 주문 결제가 기한이 지났습니다.)

c) On March 24, we informed you that outstanding balance of our invoice No. 223 (dated March 15) was not yet collected. Still, we have not heard from you.
(3월 24일에 3월 15일자 송장번호 223호에 근거한 미지급 잔액에 대한 결제가 아직 행하여지지 않음을 통보 드렸습니다. 그러나 아직 귀사로부터 아무런 연락을 못 받고 있습니다.)

2) 지불 독촉과 관련될 서류를 동봉함을 알린다.

a) Would you please make payment as soon as you can?
(조속히 지불을 부탁드립니다.)

b) Would you please settle your account or inform us why you have not paid?
(결제를 하시든지 아니면 미지불에 대한 이유를 통보해 주십시오.)

c) Please disregard this notice if payment has already been made.
(이미 지불이 되었다면 이 통지를 무시하십시오.)

d) We are enclosing copies of your P.O. and our invoice.
(귀사의 구매주문서와 당사의 송장 사본을 동봉합니다.)

e) Would you please send payment right away? Otherwise, we will not be able to accept your order.
(조속히 지불되지 않은 시 귀사의 주문을 받아들일 수 없습니다.)

f) Please confirm when you are planning to make the payment.
(언제 지불할 수 있는지 확인해 주십시오.)

Sample letter

DMS Korea

DMS Korea Co., Inc.

321 Myoung-dong, Chung-ku, Seoul 130-040, Korea

Phone: 02-570-2121/ Fax: 02-570-2122/ Email: Goodnaturekorea@Korea.com

Amherst, Inc.
East 55 Lexington Avenue
Manhattan, New York, NY10050.
phone:(212)556-1234
Fax:(212)556-1235

Dear Sirs,

Unfortunately, we have not yet received payment on our invoice No. 223 (dated March 24).

Would you please make payment as soon as you can and let us know the payment date?

Enclosed are copies of your purchase order and our invoice. Please excuse us if payment has already been made.

Sincerely,

signature

____

MIN-SHIK CHUNG
Export Manager

Writing Practice

3월 24일에 3월 15일자 송장번호 223호에 근거한 지불이 아직 행하여지지 않음을 통보 드렸습니다. 그러나 아직 귀사로부터 회신을 못 받았습니다. 아직 지불되지 않았으며, 언제쯤 지불 가능하지를 통보해 주십시오. 만약 이미 지불되었다면 이 통지를 무시하십시오.

26. 신용장(L/C: Letter of Credit)

무역거래의 대금결제의 원활함을 위해 수입업자가 자신의 거래은행(신용장 개설은행)에 신용장 개설을 의뢰하고, 신용장 개설은행이 수출업자에게 신용장에 명시된 조건과 필요한 운송서류를 제시했을 때 수출업자가 발행한 환어음을 인수, 지급 또는 매입하겠다는 약정서이다. 수출업자는 신용장을 통해 수출어음을 자신의 거래은행이 매수해 줌으로써 대금회수를 원활히 할 수 있다는 장점이 있다.

26.1 신용장거래의 참여 요소

가. 신용장개설 의뢰인 (applicant or accountee) : 물품을 수입하기 위해 자신의 거래은행에 무역거래에 입각해 신용장 발행을 의뢰하는 수입업자를 말한다.

참고

	수출업자(exporter)	수입업자(importer)
신용장거래시	수익자(beneficiary)	발행의뢰인(applicant)
선적시	선적인(shipper)	개설인(opener)
매매시	매도자(seller)	매수인(buyer)
대금결제시	대금영수인(accounter)	대금결제인(accountee)
환어음발행시	발행인(drawer)	지급인(drawee)
화물에 대해	송화인(consigner)	수화인(consignee)
신용관계	신용수령인(accreditee)	신용수취매입인(accrediter)

나. 신용장발행 은행 (issuing bank, opening bank): 개설 의뢰인의 요청과 지시에 따라 수출업자 앞으로 신용장을 발행하는 은행으로서 credit writing bank, grantor라고도 한다.

다. 통지은행 (advising bank, notifying bank): 신용장 개설은행은 신용장을 개설하면 그 사실과 내용을 수출업자에게 통지해야 한다. 신용장의 통지방법은 첫째 수익자에게 직접 통지하는 방법, 둘째 수익자 소재지에 있는 개설은행의 환거래은행을 통해 통지하는 방법이 있다. 후자의 경우 개설은행의 요청을 받아 신용장을 통지해 주는 은행을 신용장 통지은행이라 한다. 통지은행은 개설은행의 요청에 의하여 신용장이 개설되었음을 단순히 통지하는데 그치며, 거래에 대하여 어떠한 책임을 지거나 또는 약정을 하는 것은 결코 아니다.

라. 수익자 (beneficiary): 신용장에 근거해 수출대금을 취득하는 사람, 즉 수출업자를 가리킨다.

마. 매입은행 (negotiation bank): 수출자로부터 신용장의 내용과 일치하는 화물환어음을 매수하는 은행을 매입은행이라 부른다. 이 매입은행은 수출자의 거래은행이며 통지은행(advising bank)이 되는 경우가 많다.

바. 결제은행 (settling bank): 신용장의 결제통화가 수입국이나 수출국의 통화가 아닌 제3국의 통화일 경우는 제3국에 있는 개설은행의 예치환거래은행에 결제은행(settling bank)이 되며, 어음을 매입한 은행에 대금을 상환해 주는 은행이라고 해서 상환은행(reimbursing bank)이라고도 한다.

(참고) 수입신용장 개설신청서 예

<table>
<tr><th colspan="5">APPLICATION AND AGREEMENT FOR IRREVOCABLE DOCUMENTS OF CREDIT</th></tr>
<tr><td colspan="2">Please advise by ①
■ Air mail ■ Brief telex, and air mail
■ Telex/Cable</td><td colspan="3">Number ②
No. 1245</td></tr>
<tr><td colspan="2">I/L number ③
E-0111-35-003</td><td colspan="3">Date and Place of expiry ④
May 30, 2016 in New York</td></tr>
<tr><td colspan="2">Applicant ⑤
Daehan Trading Corporation
321 Sinsa-dong, Kangnam-ku
Seoul, Korea</td><td colspan="3">Beneficiary ⑥
M&M Co., Inc.
East 55 Lexington Avenue
New York, NY10050</td></tr>
<tr><td colspan="2">Advising Bank ⑦
Bank of New York</td><td colspan="3" rowspan="2">Amount ⑧
US$4,158.00(say, U.S. Dollars four million one hundred and fifty eight thousand)</td></tr>
<tr><td colspan="2">Settling Bank ⑨
The First Bank</td></tr>
<tr><td colspan="2">Partial Shipment ⑩
■ allowed
■ not allowed</td><td colspan="3" rowspan="2">Transshipment ⑪
■ allowed Tenor of draft/payment ⑮
■ not allowed
■ Banker's usance L/C
■ Shipper's usance L/C
■ Domestic usance L/C</td></tr>
<tr><td colspan="2">Loading on Board/dispatch/taking in charge from/at ⑫ New York
not later than April 20, 2016 ⑬
for transportation to Seoul, Korea ⑭</td></tr>
<tr><td colspan="5">DOCUMENTS:
⑯ ■ Signed commercial invoice in 3 fold
⑰ ■ Full set of clean on board ocean of lading made out to the of The First Bank marked 'Freight Prepaid' and 'Notify Accountee'
⑱ ■ Airway bill consigned to The First Bank marked 'Freight and notify'
⑲ ■ Insurance policy or certificate in duplicate, endorsed in blank for 11% of the invoice value, expressly stipulating that claims are payable in and it must include:
⑳ ■ Packing list in 3 fold
㉑ ■ Covering</td></tr>
<tr><td>Code No.
5005-0300123-556</td><td>Name of commodity
Red-11660n
Compact Disc Player</td><td>Quantity
154</td><td>Unit price
@US$27.00</td><td>Amount
C&F New York
US$4,158.00 U.S.A. Origin</td></tr>
<tr><td colspan="5">Special conditions and other required documents (if any): ㉒
Unless otherwise expressly stated, all banking commissions and charges outside Korea are for account of ㉓Beneficiary.
Documents to be presented within 10 ㉔ days after the date of issuance of the transport documents but within the validity of the credit.
This Documentary Credit is subject to the Unifiorm Customs and Practice for Documentary Credits
Revision, Interantional Chamber of Commerce, Paris, France. (Publication No. 400) ㉕</td></tr>
<tr><td colspan="5">상기 사항이 수입허가(승인) 사항과 상위 없음을 서약하고 위와 같은 신용장 발행을 신청하오면 배면에 기재된 담보차입증 및 신용장거래 약정서의 각 조항을 무위 준수할 것을 확약합니다.

2016년 3월 23일</td></tr>
</table>

(설명) 수입신용장 개설신청서의 기재내용

(1) airmail /cable (신용장통지방법)

(2) credit number (신용장번호)

(3) I/L No. (=import license number) (수입승인서번호)

(4) Expiry date (신용장 유효기일 및 장소)

(5) Applicant (의뢰인 혹은 신청인)

(6) Beneficiary (수혜자 혹은 수익자)

(7) Advising bank (신용장 통지은행)

(8) Amount (신용장금액 혹은 어음발행한도금액)

(9) Settling bank (대금결제은행)

(10) Partial Shipment (분할선적)

(11) Transshipment (환적)

(12) Loading on Board/dispatch/ taking in charge from/ at (상품의 선적, 발송, 수탁장소)

(13) not later than (상품의 선적, 발송, 수탁의 최종일자)

(14) for transportation (상품의 도착지항)

(15) Tenor of draft/ payment (환어음 지불기한)

(16) Signed commercial invoice in _____ fold (서명된 상업송장 ______ 부)

(17) Full set of clean on board ocean bills of lading made out to the order of the First Bank marked 'Freight': prepaid/ collect, and 'Notify Accountee' (제일은행의 지시식으로 작성된 무고장선적해상 선하증권 전품, 운임에 대한 선지불 혹은 후지불을 표기한다. Notify뒤에는 신용장의 의뢰인 즉 수입업자를 기입한다: CIF나 C&F인 경우에는 수출업자가 운임을 선급한 다음 선박회사로부터 선하증권을 발급받으므로 'prepaid'에, FOB의 경우에는 수입업자가 선박수배를 하므로 운임착불 즉 후불지급을 하므로 'collect'에 각각 표기한다.)

(18) Airway bill consigned to the First Bank marked 'Freight'" prepaid/ collect, and 'Notify Accountee' (제일은행에 송화된 항공화물운송장, (17)과 동일하게 'Freight'뒤에 'prepaid'와 'collect'를 기입하고, 'Notify'뒤는 선박회사나 포워더가 화물의 도착을 통보해주는 대상으로서 통상적으로 수입업자를 통지인으로 지정한다.)

(19) Marine insurance policy or certificate in duplicate, endorsed in blank for 110% of the invoice value, expressly stipulating that claims are payable in ____ and it must include: (해상보험을 명사하는 란으로 CIF인 경우는 수입지까지 운송료와 보험료를 수입업자가 불입하므로 해당되나, FOB인 경우는 수입지까지 공란으로 남겨둔다. Payable in 뒤에는 보험금지급지를 표기하고 include 뒤에는 보험조건을 적는다.)

(20) Packing list in _____ fold (포장명세서 _____ 부)

(21) Covering (해당 상품을 서술한다.)

(22) Special conditions and other required documents (if any) (별도의 조건들 표기)

(23) Unless otherwise expressly stated, all banking commissions and charges outside Korean are for account of beneficiary. (한국 이외에서 발생하는 모든 은행수수료나 비용의 부담자인 수익자를 기입한다.)

(24) Documents to be presented within ____ days after the date of issuance of the transport documents but within the validity of the credit. (선적서류 제시기한을 표기하는 란으로 은행은 통상 7 – 14일 정도로 잡지만, 신용장에 제출기한이 명시되는 않으면 선하증권이나 운송서류의 발송 후 21일까지만 인정한다.)

(25) This Documentary Credit is subject to the Uniform Customs and Practice for Documentary Credits (1983 Revision, International Chamber of Commerce, Paris, France, Publication No. 400) (화환신용장에 관한 통일규칙 및 관례 (1983년 개정), 또한 국제상업회의소 간행 제 400호)

A Letter of Credit 예

Inter-American Development Bank[1)]
229 est 43rd Street
New York, NY 10036
Phone : (212) 556-1234
Fax : (212) 556-1235

August 21, 2016[2)]

To : Daehan Trading Corporation
321 Sinsa-dong, Kangnam-gu, Seoul, Korea[3)]

This credit is being advised
by AIR MAIL
Through : The First Bak of
Seoul, Korea[4)]

Letter of Credit No. E-0111-35-003[5)]

Dear Sirs :

We hereby open our irrevocable without recourse letter of credit[6)] in your favor for account of[7)] M&M Co., Inc., New York for a sum or sums not exceeding a total of U.S. $4,158.00[8)] available by your draft(s) at sight[9)] on the First Bank of Seoul, Korea,[10)] for 100% of invoice cost[11)] to be accompanied by following[12)] documents evidencing shipment(s) of[13)]

154 units of RCD-1600N Compact Disc Player, @U.S. $27.00, Korea Origin, C&F New York from Incheon, Korea to New York, U.S.A.[14)]
Full set of clean on board ocean bills of lading[15)] made out to the order of[16)] the First Bank. Marked "FREIGHT Prepaid"[17)] and "Notify the accountee".[18)]
Marine insurance policy or certificate[19)] in duplicate, endorsed in blank for 110% of the invoice value.[20)]
Insurance policies or certificates must expressly stipulate that claims are payable in the currency of the draft[21)] and policies or certificates must also indicate a claims setting agent in U.S.A.[22)] Insurance must include :
Institute cargo clause :[23)]
Signed commercial invoice[24)] in quintuplicate.
Packing list[25)] in quintuplicate.
Consular invoice and certificate of origin in dupiicate issued or visaed by American consul.
Partial shipments[26)] are prohibited. Transshipment[27)] is prohibited.
Shipment must be effected on or before November 3, 2016.[28)]
Draft(s) must be presented for payment/negotiation on or before November 8, 2016.[29)]

All draft(s) hereunder[30] must be marked "Drawn under Inter-American Development Bank, Credit No. E-0111-35-003 dated May 30, 2016"[31] and all other documents shall also contain the reference number of this credit.
This amount and date of negotiation[32] of each draft must be endorsed on reverse side hereof the negotiating Bank. We hereby agree[33] with the drawers, endorsers, and bona fide holders of drafts drawn under and in compliance with the terms of this Credit that the same shall be duly honored on due presentation.[34]

Unless otherwise expressly stated, this credit is subject to "uniform Customs and Practice for documentary Credits (1993 Revision), Internatinal Chamber of Commerce Publication No. 500."

Sincerely Yours,

Inter-American Development Bank

____

Authorized Signaature

(설명) 신용장 기재내용

1) 신용장 개설은행(issuing bank)
2) 신용장 개설 일자 (issuing date)
3) 수익자(beneficiary) 혹은 수출업자의 주소
4) 통지방법과 통지은행(advising bank)
5) 신용장 번호
6) irrevocable without recourse letter of credit 상환청구불능 취소불능 신용장
7) in your favor form account of Amherst, Inc. 신용장을 개설 의뢰자인 Amherst, Inc. 계정으로 귀사를 수취인으로 하며(Amherst, Inc.는 수입업체이며, in you favor에서 your는 수출업자인 DMS Korea Co., Inc.이다.)
8) For a sum or sums not exceeding a total of U.S. $4,158,000 신용장금액의 한도액
9) at sight 일람출급어음을 의미하며, 기한부어음(usance bill)일 경우에는 "at 90 days after sight"등으로 표시한다.
10) on the First Bank 어음의 피발행인(drawee) 혹은 지불인을 의미한다.
11) For 100% invoice cost 어음금액을 의미한다.
12) 새 be accompanied by 어음을 매입은행에 제시할 때 첨부되는 서류들을 의미한다.
13) evidencing shipments of 선적을 증명하는
14) 선적항과 도착항을 의미한다.
15) full set of clean on board ocean bills of lading 무고장부 선적선하증권
16) made out to the order of ...의 지시식으로 작성된
17) FREIGHT Prepaid 운임선급조건으로 체결됨을 의미한다. C&F 혹은 CIF와 같이 해상운임을 매도인이 지불하는 경우에는 신용장에 freight prepaid,라 기재하고, FOB와 같이 매수인이 해상운임을 지불하는 경우에는 신용장에 freight collect(운임착금)이라 기재한다.
18) Notify the accountee 수입업자(Amherst, Inc.)에게 통지하라.
19) marine insurance policy or certificate 해상보험증권 혹은 보험증명서
20) 110% of the invoice value 보험금액은 송장금액에 10%의 희망이익을 가산한 금액이다.

21) in the currency of the draft 어음에 표시된 것과 동일한 통화료

22) claims setting agent in U.S.A 미국에 있는 손해배상금 지급처

23) institute Cargo Clauses 협회적하약관

24) signed commercial invoice 서명필 상업송장

25) packing list 포장명세서

26) partial shipment 분할선적

27) transshipment 환적

28) shipment must be effected on or before 최종선적기일을 의미한다.

29) drafts must be presented for payment/negotiation 어음은 지불과 매도를 위해 제시된어야 한다.

30) all drafts hereunder 이 신용장에 의거해 발행된 모든 어음들

31) 한국제일은행이 2006년 5월 30일에 발행한 신용장번호 E-0111-35-003에 의거하여 발행되어야 한다.

32) the amount and date of negotiation 매입금액 및 매일일자

33) We hereby agree 이렇게 하여 ...을 당행(제일은행)은 동의한다.

34) on due presentation 정당하게 제시된 대로

26.2 신용장에 입각한 결제의 흐름(CIF계약의 경우)

가. 수출업자와 수입업자 사이에서 신용장에 따른 결제조건부의 무역계약을 맺는다.

나. 무역계약 입각하여 수입자는 거래은행에 신용장의 발행의뢰를 한다.

다. 신용장발행은행은 심사한 뒤 신용장을 통지은행을 경유하여 발행한다.

라. 통지은행은 수출업자 앞으로 신용장의 도착을 수출업자에게 통지한다.

마. 신용장이 도착하면 내용을 체크하여 화물을 선적한다.

바. 선적을 하면 선박회사에서 선하증권(bill of lading; B/L)이 교부되지만 그 외 밀 행상 보험회사와 계약할 때 교부되는 해상보험증권 또한 수출화물의 명세서인 인보이스를 갖추는데 이것을 선적서류라고 한다. 이때 수출업자는 환어음을 발행한다.

사. 환어음에 선적서류 신용장을 첨부하여 거래처 외환은행에 매수 의뢰한다. 외환은행은 신용장조건에 합치된 것이라는 확인을 하고 매수에 응한다.

아. 매수에 응하면 환어음의 대리금액을 수출업자에게 건네준다. 이때 전수한 환예약이 되어 있으면 그 예약에 맞추어 달러에서 원으로 환산된다. 이것으로 수출업자는 수출대금의 회수가 된 것으로 일단락된다.

자. 매수은행은 매수한 화물환어음 및 신용장을 신용장발행은행에 내보이고 어음대금을 회수한다. 실제는 매수은행에 있는 신용장발행은행 계좌에서 어음대금을 마음대로 유용하는 경우가 많다.

차. 신용장발행은행은 환어음을 수입업자에게 내보인다.

카. 수입자는 어음대금을 신용장 발행은행에 지불한다.

타. 신용장발행은행은 수입업자의 어음대금지불과 교환으로 선적서류를 인도한다. 특히 선하증권은 수입화물이 구체화된 것이기 때문에 이것이 없으면 선박회사에서 화물을 인수할 수 없다. 또한 신용장 발행은행은 수입자에게 대해 어음 대금결제를 위한 융자를 행하는 경우도 있다.

파. 수입업자는 은행에서 받은 선하증권을 선박회사에 제출한다.

하. 선박회사는 제시한 선하증권과 교환으로 선적된 화물을 수입자에게 인도한다. 이것으로 수입자 앞으로 무사히 수입화물이 인도되는 것이다. 그래서 수입국에서 통관수속을 하고 수입국 당국의 수입허가를 얻은 후 수입국 내에 유통하게 된다.

26.3 신용장의 종류

가. 취소불능신용장(irrevocable L/C)과 취소가능신용장(revocable L/C)

발행은행이 일방적으로 수익자에게 신용장의 변경취소를 행할 수 있는 취소가능 신용장이라 하는데 이는 수익자(수출업자)에게는 대단한 위험이 따른다. 반면, 신용장을 발행하여 수익자에게 통지한 후에는 신용장관계당사자인 수익자나 확인은행 등 전원의 동의없이 취소 또는 철회할 수 없는 신용장을 취소불능신용장이라 한다.

나. 확인신용장(confirmed credit)

개설은행과 별도로 확인은행이 대금지급을 보증하는 신용장으로 발행은행이 사고 등에 의해 지불불능에 빠져도 확인은행(보통 통지은행과 일치)은 어음의 지불을 거절하지 못하는 신용장이므로 수익자(수출업자)에게는 안전하다.

다. 양도가능신용장 (transferable credit)

신용장금액의 전부 또는 일부를 수익자가 제 3자에게 양도할 수 있는 신용장이다.

26.4 신용장 조건 변경(L/C Amendment) 및 취소(L/C Cancellation)

신용장의 내용을 어떤 사정으로 인하여 변경하거나 효력을 소멸시키기 위하여 유효기간 내에 개설은행, 수익자, 개설의뢰인, 확인은행 등의 모든 거래 당사자들의 합의가 있어야 한다.

26.5 신용장상의 용어해석

about/ approximately/ circa 과부족 허용한도 +/- 10% 수익

promptly/ as soon as possible/ immediately 즉시

on or about 기재된 일자 전후 각 5일 (총 11일)

to/ until/ from 당일 포함

after 당일 제외

during the first half 양단일 포함 1일-15일 동안

during the second half 양단일 포함 16일-말일 동안

at the beginning of this month 양단일 포함 1일-10일

at the middle of this month 양단일 포함 11일-20일

at the end of 양단일 포함 21일-말일

27. 무신용장 거래방식

신용장거래 방식은 불확실한 수입업자의 신용을 확실한 은행의 신용으로 전환하여 줌으로써 대금결제에 대한 책임을 은행이 지는데 반하여, 무신용장거래방식은 수출입거래 당사자 간의 무역거래만으로 이루어지면 은행은 이에 대한 책임을 지지 않으므로 대금회수가 다소 어려울 수 있다. 최근 교역량의 증가와 수출거래처의 다변화 등으로 무신용장거래가 점차 증가하고 있다. 무신용장거래 방식은 D/A(Document against Acceptance)와 D/P(documents against payment)는 모두 수출업자의 입장에서 보면 모두 수출을 하고 난 뒤에 대금을 회수할 수 있다.

27.1 D/P (Documents against Payment: 지급인도조건 추심거래방식)

수출업자가 수입업자와의 매매계약에 따라 물품을 자신의 책임 하에 선적한 후, 관련서류가 첨부된 일람출급어음(at-sight draft)을 수입업자를 지급인으로 발행하여 자신의 거래은행에 제출하면, 해당 은행은 운송서류와 함께 첨부된 환어음을 수입업자 거래은행에 송부한다. 수입업자 거래은행은 수입업자에게 대금을 지급받고 서류를 인도한다. 지급받은 대금을 수출업자의 거래은행으로 송금하는 결제 방식이다.

27.2 D/A (Documents against Acceptance: 인수인도조건 추심거래방식)

수입업자의 거래은행이 수입업자에게 환어음(usance draft)을 제시하였을 때, 수입업자는 은행으로부터 운송서류를 인도받고 환어음을 인수하나 이때 어음금액을 은행에 지불하지 않고 만기일에 지급하게 되는 외상거래이다. 수입업자에게 환어음의 지급만기일 만큼 D/P방식보다 더 오랜 기간 동안 신용을 공여한다.

Sample letter 1

(D/A조건으로 수출업자가 수입업자에게 보내는 서신)

Dear Sirs:

We are pleased to inform you that arrangements have now been made to ship the dress goods you ordered on 15 October. The consignment will leave London on 1 November, due to arrive at Quebec on the 22nd.

Based on our usual terms of payment we have drawn on you at 60 days and passed the draft and shipping documents to our bankers. The documents will be presented to ou by the National Bank of Canada against your acceptance of the draft in the usual way.

We hope that you will find our conditions and terms satisfactory.

Yours sincerely,

(해석)

귀하가 10월 15일 주문하신 드레스품목을 선적하기 위한 모든 준비가 완료됐음을 알려드립니다. 탁송물은 11월 1일 런던을 출발하여 22일에 퀘벡에 도착할 예정입니다.
우리의 통상 지불조건에 기초해 일람후 60일짜리 어음을 당사로 발행했으며 환어음과 선적서류를 은행에 제출했습니다. 그 서류들은 인수인도방식으로 카나다은행에 의해 귀사에 제시될 겁니다. 우리의 모든 조건들이 만족스럽기를 빕니다.

Sample letter 2

(D/P조건으로 수출업자가 수입업자에게 보내는 서신)

Dear Sirs:

We were pleased to receive your faxed order of 29 June and have arranged to ship the electric shavers by SS Tyrania, leaving New York on 6 July and due to arrive at London on the 24th.

As the urgency of your order left no time to make the usual enquiries, we are compelled to place this transaction on a cash basis and have drawn on you through Midminster Bank Ltd. for the amount of the enclosed invoice. The bank will instruct their correspondent in London to pass the bill of lading to you against payment of the draft.

Special care has been taken to select items suited to your local conditions. We hope you will find them entirely satisfactory and that your present order will be the first of many.

Yours faithfully,

(해석)

당사는 6월 29일자 귀사 팩스로 보내주신 주문을 받고 SS Tyrania선적 편으로 전기면도기를 보낼 준비를 마쳤습니다. 그 선적은 7월 6일 뉴욕을 떠나 24일에 런던에 도착할 예정입니다. 귀사의 긴급한 주문으로 조회를 할 시간적 여유가 없었으므로 이 거래를 현금으로 할 수 밖에 없음을 알려드리며 동봉한 송장의 대금은 Midminster은행을 통해 귀사로부터 받겠습니다. 그 은행은 어음지불과 동시에 (교환하여) 선하증권을 귀사에 넘겨줄 것을 거래은행에 지시할 겁니다. 귀사의 지역적 특성에 맞는 물품을 선택하는 데 특별한 주의를 기울였습니다. 보내드리는 물품에 만족하고 앞으로도 계속적인 주문을 고대합니다.

(참고)

transaction 거래; on a cash basis ..현금거래를 기초로; correspondent 거래처(은행), 통신원; bill of lading 선하증권; take care (of) 주의하다; against 교환하여

28. 환어음 (Draft, B/E, Bill of exchange)

a. 환어음의 정의

환어음이란 국제거래상 채권자가 채무자에 대하여 그 어음상의 표시금액을 채권자가 제시할 경우 일정한 기간 및 장소에서 무조건 지급할 것을 위탁하는 유가증권에 해당한다.

b. 환어음의 발행과 지급

환어음의 발행인은 어음을 발행하고 서명하는 물품의 수출업자, 즉 신용자의 수익자가 된다. 환어음의 지급인은 일반적으로 신용장발행신청인 혹은 발행은행이 된다.

c. 환어음 지급기일과 금액

- 일람출급어음(at-sight draft): 환어음의 지급기일은 일 'at sight'으로 표시되고, 환어음이 제시되면 즉시 결제가 이루어진다.
- 기한부어음(usance draft)인 경우는 'at __ days after sight', 'at __ days after B/L date'등으로 표시된다. 신용장상의 지급인이 먼저 어음을 인수하고 인수 후 정해진 기일이 지나서 결제가 이루어진다.

(예) We have drawn on your bank at 30 days after sight for 100% invoice value under the credit No. 1435.

d. 무역어음의 인수 및 할인 기관과 어음의 할인

이와 관련된 기관은 은행, 단자, 종합금융사 등이며 인수시 수수료 (0.5-6%)나 어음할인은 수출업체의 수출실적, 생산능력 등을 고려하여 금융기관이 (통상 11.5%-12.0%) 자율적으로 결정한다.

참고 환어음의 예

BILL OF EXCHANGE

NO. ABC-123 DATE: May 30, 2017

For USD 5,780 Place: Seoul, Korea

At 30 DAYS AFTER sight of this FIRST BILL of EXCHANGE (Second of the same tenor and date being unpaid) pay to the order of the First Bank the sum of SAY US DOLLARS FIVE THOUSAND SEVEN HUNDRED EIGHTY ONLY.

Value received and charge the same to account of Amherst, Inc.

Drawn under Inter-American Development Bank

L/C No. BCO-2345432 dated April 20, 2017

To. INTER-AMERICAN DEVELOPMENT BANK OF NEW YORK, NY

DMS Korea, INC.

Signature_____________________

Export Manager

(설명) 환어음 기재 사항

1) Bill of Exchange: 환어음 표시
2) NO. : 어음번호, 후일 참조를 위해 필요
3) Date: 발행일, 외국환은행이 어음과 함께 제시된 선적서류를 매입한 날짜이며, 이는 신용장 유효기일 이내이어야 한다.
4) For: 환어음의 금액, 이는 상업송장액과 일치해야 한다.
5) Place: 발행지 표시는 환어음의 효력이 행위지 법률에 의해 처리되므로 매우 중요
6) At 30 DAYS AFTER sight of: 지급기일 (결제조건)]
7) This FIRST BILL of EXCHANGE(Second of the same tenor and date being unpaid) pay to: 어음 발행 수, 어음이 한 세트, 즉 제 1권과 제 2권으로 발행되었을 경우, 이 중 이중지급의 사고를 방지하기 위해서 "second(first) of the same tenor and date being unpaid"와 같이 표시되어 하나에 의해서 지급되면 다른 것은 자동적으로 무효가 된다는 것을 표시한다.
8) the order of the First Bank the sum of : 수취인, 이는 환어음의 발행인이 될 수도 있고 발행이 지시하는 제 3자가 될 수도 있다. 신용장 거래 시 pay to 다음에는 통상 매입은행이 기재된다. (한국제일은행이라는 지시인에게 총액을 지급하시오.)
9) SAY US DOLLARS FIVE THOUSAND SEVEN HUNDRED EIGHTY ONLY: 문자금액, 이용금액을 아라비아 숫자가 아닌 문자로 표시한다. 또한 환어음에는 반드시 화폐의 종류가 명시되어야 한다.
10) Value received and: 이는 법률상에 가치 있는 약인, 즉 보통 유통되는 증권이 아니라 어떤 상업 거래의 가치에 대한 결제임을 표시하는 문언이 된다.
11) Charge the same to account of Amherst, Inc.: 신용장상의 Accountee, 이것은 은행이 지급인에게 지시하는 내용으로서 해당 환어음이 지급인에 의하여 결제되면 그 자금은 Account of 이하에 기재되는 자로부터 지불 받으라는 의미
12) Drawn under Inter-American Development Bank: 신용장개설은행을 의미하며, D/P, D/A등 무신용장방식의 경우에는 공란 또는 계약서상 지정은행을 기재
13) L/C No. BCO-2345432: 신용장번호, D/A, D/P인 경우에는 계약서 번호를 기재한다.
14) dated April 20, 2006: 신용장 발행일자

15) To. INTER-AMERICAN DEVELOPMENT BANK, NY: 지급인(drawee)과 지급지, 지급인은 신용장개설은행이나 개설의뢰인 즉 수입업자가 될 수도 있고, 또 다른 제3의 은행이 될 수도 있다.

16) 발행인의 기명날인: 환어음을 발행하는 자는 신용장상의 수익자 또는 양도받은 경우에는 양수인이 되면 반드시 기명날인가지 해야 된다. 사용되는 발행인의 서명날인은 화환어음 약정시 은행에 제출된 서명과 일치해야 한다.

환어음 개설통지

DMS Korea, Inc.
321 Myoung-dong, Chung-ku, Seoul 130-040, Korea
Phone: 02-570-2121/ Fax: 02-570-2122
Email: Goodnaturekorea@Korea.com

Mr. Dan Slobin:
Manager
Amherst, Inc.
East 55 Lexington Avenue
Manhattan, New York, NY10050.
phone:(212)556-1234
Fax:(212)556-1235

Dear Sir,

We thank you for your order of 25 June for 1,000 meters of poplin shirting at the quoted price of $0.86 per metre.

The shirting is now ready for despatch and will be shipped by the Daehanho, sailing from New York on July !8.

We are pleased to enclose shipping documents. Also enclosed is our sight draft drawn at 30 days as agreed. Please accept and return it immediately.

Yours faithfully,
signature

MIN-SHIK CHUNG
Export Manager

(해석)

당사는 미터 당 0.86달러의 견적가격에 포프린 셔츠감 1,000미터를 6월 25일자로 주문해 주셔서 감사드립니다. 그 셔츠감은 운송준비를 마치었고, 7월 18일자로 뉴욕을 출발하는 대한호에 의해 수송될 겁니다. 선적서류를 동봉하며 또한 동의된 대로 일람후 30일로 발행된 일람어음을 동봉합니다. 결제하는 즉시 반송해 주십시오.

29. 송장(invoice)

원칙적으로 수출업자 (신용장 수익자, 운송의뢰인(consignor))가 수입업자 (신용장개설 신청인, 수화인(consignee))에게 보내는 선적화물에 대한 내용명세서 겸 대금청구서이다. 수입업자는 송장내용에 따라 수입화물에 대한 내용을 처리하게 되며 화물이 도착했을 때 수입통관이 이루어진다. 송장은 거래계약의 이행과정을 모두 보여주므로 문제발생시 중요한 입증자료가 된다.

<table>
<tr><th colspan="6">Commercial Invoice</th></tr>
<tr><td colspan="3" rowspan="2">① Shipper/Exporter
Daehan Trading Corperation
321 Sinsa-dong, Kangnam-gu
Seoul, Korea</td><td colspan="3">⑦ No. & Date of invoice
ABC-113-23 May 3, 2016</td></tr>
<tr><td colspan="3">⑧ No. & Date of L/C
E-o111-35-003 May 1, 2016</td></tr>
<tr><td colspan="3" rowspan="2">② For account & rist of Messrs.
M&M Co., Inc.
East 55 Lexington Avenue
New York, NY10050</td><td colspan="3">⑨ Buyer (if other than cousignee)</td></tr>
<tr><td colspan="3">⑩ Remarks :</td></tr>
<tr><td colspan="2">③ Port of Loading
PUSAN, KOREA</td><td>④ Final Destination
New York, U.S.A.</td><td colspan="3" rowspan="2">⑪ Terms of delivery and payment</td></tr>
<tr><td colspan="2">⑤ Carrier
DAEHANDHO</td><td>⑥ Sailing on or about
March 30, 2016</td></tr>
<tr><td>⑫ Shipping Marks</td><td>⑬ No. & Kind
Kind of pkgs</td><td>⑭ Description of goods
RCD-1660N Compact Disc Player</td><td>⑮ Quantity/ Unit
154</td><td>⑯ Unit-Price
USD 27.00</td><td>⑰ Amount
C&F NEW York, U.S.A.
USD 4,158.00</td></tr>
<tr><td colspan="3">Cable address : DAEHAN, SEOUL
Telex code : TYCEMEN K27541
Telephone : (02) 570-2121</td><td colspan="3">Daehan Trading Co.
Signature
Export Manager</td></tr>
</table>

(설명) 송장기재 요령

1) Shipper/Exporter: 매도인 또는 수출업자 이름과 주소 기재
2) Consignee: 물품을 인도받을 매수자 또는 수입업자의 이름과 주소를 기재하며, 이는 선하증권에 기재될 매수인과 동일
3) From: 출발예정 항구, 공항 등의 명칭을 기재, 이는 신용장 또는 계약서상의 적재지(place of loading)와 일치해야 한다.
4) To: 최종 목적지인 항구, 공항 등의 명칭을 기재, 이는 신용장 또는 계약서상의 도착지완 일치해야 한다.
5) Vessel/Flight:운송에 사용되는 선박/비행기 명칭을 기재
6) Departure Date: 화물을 적재한 선박이나 비행기의 출발일자를 기재, 송장 작성시점에서는 선적 일자를 정확히 알 수 없으므로 예상되는 선적일자의 7일 전후로 기재
7) Invoice No. and Date: 매도인이 상업송장에 기재한 참조번호 및 송장발행일
8) L/C No. and Date: 신용장 번호 및 발행일
9) Buyer(if other than consignee): 상품을 구매한 개인 또는 법인의 이름과 주서
10) other reference or Remarks: 기타 참조사항, 거래 상대방이 신용장이나 계약서에서 별도로 요구한 사항을 기재
11) Terms of Delivery and Payment: 인도조건과 지불조건을 기재하며 지불조건은 INCOTERMS와 같은 조건을 따른다. 사용통화를 명기한다.
12) Shipping Marks: 선적하인 표시
13) No. & Kind of Packages: 포장 종류 당 포장화물의 개수와 각 물품의 포장형태 기재
14) Goods Description: 물품명세서는 규격(specification), 품질(quality), 등급(grade)등 해당 물품에 대한 정확한 명세를 기재
15) Quantity: 송장금액 계산의 기초가 되는 최소단위당 수량을 기재, 수량의 계산단위는 일반적으로 다음과 같이 개수 혹은 도량형에 의하여 계산된다.
16) Unit Price: 단위 수량 당 가격
17) Amount: 단위당 단가에 수량을 곱한 총금액
18) Signed by: 송장작성자의 서명

19) 차변증서(debit note)와 대변증서(credit note)

수출업자가 수입업자에게 적정 가격 이하로 금액을 청구한 경우, 그에 해당하는 금액의 차변증서를 발송한다. 수입업자는 청구금액을 송금한다.

수출업자가 수입업자에게 적정 가격 이상으로 금액을 청구거나 수입업자가 물품을 반송한 경우 수출업자를 수입업자에게 가격부과를 취소하는 대변증서를 발송한다.

30. 기타서신

30.1 방문계획서신

내용
1) 방문예정일을 알린다. 2) 상대 회사에 방문 의사를 밝힌다. 3) 방문 목적을 알린다. 4) 편리한 날짜를 확인한다.

표현연습
1) 방문예정일을 알린다. a) I am planning to visit New York from March 24 to March 26. (저는 3월 24일부터 3월 26일까지 뉴욕 방문을 계획하고 있습니다.) b) I am planning to visit New York between March 24 and March 26. (저는 3월 24일과 3월 26일 사이에 뉴욕방문을 계획하고 있습니다.) c) I am scheduled to go to New York to attend an annual meeting. (저는 연례회의 참석을 위해 뉴욕 방문을 예정하고 있습니다.)
2) 상대 회사에 방문 의사를 밝힌다. a) ... and would like to meet with you. (귀하를 뵙고 싶습니다.) b) ... and would like to visit you during this time. (이 기간 동안 귀하를 뵙기를 원합니다.) c) ... and would like to visit you for one day between March 24 and March 26. (3월 24일과 3월 26일 중간 하루에 당신을 귀사를 방문하기를 원합니다.)
3) 방문 목적을 알린다. a) The purpose would be to discuss (review) the sales plan (sales possibilities). (이번 목적은 판매계획(판매 가능성)을 논의 (재검토)하기 위한 것입니다.) b) The purpose would be to introduce (demonstrate) our new products. (이번 목적은 당사의 신형 상품을 소개 (설명)드리는 것입니다.) c) This purpose is to prepare for the exhibition. (이번 목적은 전시회 준비를 위한 것입니다.)

4) 편리한 날짜를 확인한다.

a) Would you please let me know which day would be convenient for you?
(귀하께서 편리한 날짜를 알려주세요.)

b) Could you please advise me the date by fax if either March 24 or March 25 would be convenient for you?
(3월 24일이나 3월 25일 중 편리한 날짜를 팩스로 알려주세요.)

Sample letter

DMS Korea

DMS Korea Co., Inc.
321 Myoung-dong, Chung-ku, Seoul 130-040, Korea
Phone: 02-570-2121/ Fax: 02-570-2122/ Email: Goodnaturekorea@Korea.com

Amherst, Inc.
East 55 Lexington Avenue
Manhattan, New York, NY10050
phone:(212)556-1234
Fax:(212)556-1235

Dear Sirs,

I will be in the U.S.A. on March 24 to attend an annual meeting at Hilton Hotel, Manhattan, New York.

Since I'll be staying there for one week, would it be possible to visit you during this time? The purpose would be to discuss the possibility of opening a business relation with your company.

Could you please let me know the date by fax if either March 24 or March 25 would be convenient for you?

I am looking forward to your reply.

Sincerely yours,

signature

____
MIN-SHIK CHUNG
Manager

30.2 방문계획 회신

내용

1) 서신 수취를 확인한다.

2) 방문 계획에 대해 감사함을 표한다.

3) 맺음말을 한다.

표현연습

1) 서신 수취를 확인한다.

a) Thank you very much for your letter of March 10.
(3월 10일자 귀하 서신에 감사드립니다.)

b) I received your letter of March 10.
(3월 10일자 귀하 서신을 받았습니다.)

2) 방문 계획에 대해 감사함을 표한다.

a) We would like to welcome you.
(귀하의 방문을 환영합니다.)

b) We would be very happy to welcome you.
(귀하의 방문을 환영합니다.)

c) Your visit is always welcome.
(귀하의 방문은 언제든지 환영입니다.)

d) I will be waiting for you at noon on March 14.
(3월 14일 정오에 귀하를 기다리겠습니다.)

e) I would be pleased if you could visit us on March 24.
(본사를 3월 24일에 방문해 주십시오.)

f) Would you please let us know your itinerary (schedule/ flight information/ arrival time)?
(귀하의 여행일정(스케줄/ 비행정보/ 도착시간)을 알려주세요.)

g) Please give me a call at 212-443-5252 as soon as you have arrived.
(도착 즉시 저희에게 전화주세요.)

h) Please call me as soon as you arrive at Hilton Hotel. My telephone number is 212-443-5252.
(Hilton호텔에 도착하자마다 전화주세요.)

i) Our staff will be waiting for you at the airport.
(당사 직원이 공항에서 귀하를 마중할 것입니다.)

3) 맺음말을 한다.

a) I hope you will have a good trip.
(좋은 여행이 되기를 바랍니다.)

b) I am looking forward to seeing you soon.
(곧 뵐 수 있기를 고대합니다.)

c) I wish you a safe trip to U.S and look forward to seeing you.
(미국까지 안전한 여행되시고 귀하를 뵙기를 고대합니다.)

d) If you have any questions, please do not hesitate to let me know.
(질문이 있으면 주저 말고 연락주세요.)

Sample letter

Amherst, Inc
East 55 Lexington Avenue, Manhattan, New York, NY10050
phone:(212)556-1234/ Fax:(212)556-1235/ mandmco@finance.com

DMS Korea, Inc.
321 Myoung-dong, Chung-ku
Seoul 130-040, Korea
Phone: 02-570-2121
Fax: 02-570-2122

Dear Sirs,

Thank you for your letter of March 10, 2017.

We would be happy to welcome you from March 15 to March 20. In the meantime, would you please send us your itinerary, flight information, and arrival time? Also, could you let us know where you will be staying?

When you receive this information, we will arrange to have someone to meet you at the airport.

Sincerely yours,

signature

____

DON SLOBIN
Manager

30.3 방문일자 변경 요청 서신

내용

1) 서신 수취를 확인한다.

2) 방문일자 변경 이유와 방문 가능한 날짜를 통보한다.

3) 맺음말을 한다.

표현연습

1) 서신 수취를 확인한다.

a) Thank you very much for your letter of March 24, 2017.
(2017년 3월 24일 서신 감사드립니다.)

2) 방문일자 변경 이유와 방문 가능한 날짜를 통보한다.

a) Unfortunately, I cannot see you on March 24 because of a business trip.
(유감스럽게도 출장으로 3월 24일 귀하를 뵐 수가 없습니다.)

b) March 24 will be convenient for us.
(3월 24일이 저희에게는 편리한 날짜입니다.)

c) Would you please change the date to March 24?
(3월 24일로 날짜를 변경해 주시겠습니까?)

d) Otherwise (If not), please let me know what date and time would be convenient for you?
(그렇지 않으면 귀하의 편리한 날짜와 시간을 알려주세요.)

3) 맺음말을 한다.

a) I am looking forward to receiving your mail.

Sample letter

DMS Korea

DMS Korea, Inc.
321 Myoung-dong, Chung-ku, Seoul 130-040, Korea
Phone: 02-570-2121/ Fax: 02-570-2122/ Email: Goodnaturekorea@Korea.com

Amherst, Inc.
East 55 Lexington Avenue
Manhattan, New York, NY10050
phone:(212)556-1234
Fax:(212)556-1235

Dear Sirs,

Thank you very much for your letter of March 24, 2017.

Unfortunately, I cannot see you on March 20 because of a rather tight schedule. However, March 21 would be perfect. Could you change the date to March 21? If not, could you consider another date that would be convenient for you?

I am looking forward to receiving your mail.

Sincerely yours,

signature

____

MIN-SHIK CHUNG
Manager

31. 팩스(Fax)

1) 팩스는 일반 서신과 유사한 형식을 취한다. 팩스 송신표(cover sheet)는 일반 서신용지나 자사의 필요한 정보를 담고 있는 letterhead 용지를 사용한다.
2) 팩스내용은 타이핑하는 것이 보통이나, 내용이 간단하거나 비격식 내용은 수기(handwriting)를 하기도 한다.
3) 팩스내용은 사본이므로 실제 서명이 필요한 경우는 별도로 원본을 송달해야 한다.
4) 여러 팩스내용들이 섞이는 혼동을 피하기 위해 페이지 수를 반드시 적어 넣는다.

(예) Pages: This + 2 (total 3 pages)
Pages: Cover plus 1 (total 2 pages)
Pages: This only (total 1 page)
Pages: 3 (total 3 pages)

5) 팩스내용은 A4지 1매 혹은 2매 정도의 분량으로 간결해야 한다.

FAX COVER SHEET

DMS Korea, Inc.
321 Myoung-dong, Chung-ku, Seoul 130-040, Korea
Phone: 82-2-570-2121/ Fax: 82-2-570-2122

TO: Amherst, Inc.
ATTN: Don Slobin, Export Manager
FAX NO: 1-212-556-7389
DATE: March 10, 2017
REF:
PAGES: This only
MESSAGES:

Dear sir,

Visiting on March 20
Thank you very much for your letter of February 24.

Unfortunately, I cannot see you on March 20 because of a rather tight schedule. However, March 21 would be perfect. Could you change the date to March 21? If not, could you consider another date that would be convenient for you?

I am looking forward to receiving your mail.

Sincerely yours,

signature

____
Min-SHIK CHUNG
Manager

(참고) Fax에 자주 사용되는 약어들

ABT	about	관하여
ACPT	accept	결제하다
ADV	advise	통지하다
AGN	again	다시
AKA	also known as	다른 이름으로, 별칭으로
ASAP	as soon as possible	가능한 빨리
ATTN	attention	특정인 열람
BTW	by the way	그런데
DOB	date of birth	출생일
ETA	estimated time of arrival	추정되는 도착 시간
ETD	estimated time of departure	추정되는 출발 시간
FAQ	frequently asked questions	빈번한 질문
FY	for your information	참고로
IAE	in any event	어쨌든
IOW	in other words	다시 말해서
IMO	in my opinion	내 견해로
NRN	no response needed	답장 불필요
OIC	Oh! I see.	아! 알았어요.
OTOH	on the other hand	다른 한편으로
PLS	please	제발
QLTY	quality	품질
QNTY	quantity	수량
SMPL	sample	견본
SPEC	specification	제품사양
TIA	thank in advance	미리 감사드립니다
TYVM	thank you very much	매우 감사합니다
VIP	very important person	주요인사
WRT	with respect to	관하여

32. 전자메일 (E-mail)

E-mail(Email/ Electronic mail)은 무역거래의 신속함 때문에 오늘날 많이 사용되고 있다. 서식이나 스타일 면에서 일반 서신과 유사하나, 격식에 덜 얽매인다든지 구어체에 가까운 표현이 사용된다는 점에서 서신 보다 좀 더 자유롭게 사용된다

sample E-mail

① Delete ② Reply ③ Forward ④ Spam ⑤ Attachment
⑥ From : kskim@gmail.com ⑦ To: Danslobin@mandm.com
⑧ CC : support@mandm.cm
⑨ BCC : gspark@hotmail.com
⑩ SUBJECT : PRICES
⑪ Dear Sir/Madam ⑫ Please can you send me a price list of your service agents on the US. ⑬ Yours, ⑭ K.S. KIM

1) Delete: 삭제 기능
2) Reply: 회신 기능, 회신할 때: E-mail의 회신을 보낼 때, Reply 기능을 사용할 수도 있지만 이보다 메일을 새로 작성하는 것이 좋다. 회신기능을 이용할 경우 수신된 메일 내용이 뒤에 그대로 이어지기 때문이다. 수신된 메일 내용이 반드시 필요할 경우에는 주제에 해당하는 부분만을 이용하든지, 아니면 수신된 불필요한 부분은 삭제하고 [snip] 혹은 [deleted](중략)을 적어 넣는 것이 바람직하다.
3) Forward: 회람 기능, 주로 수신된 메일을 다른 사람들에게 보낼 때 사용
4) Spam: 스팸메일 처리기능으로 SPAM MAIL은 필요한 정보를 한번에 다수의 상대에게 보내지는 이메일이며, 주로 일방적으로 보내져 오는 광고 등의 불필요한 메일들이 이에 해당

5) Attachment: 자료 첨부 기능

6) From: 보내는 사람의 이메일 주소

7) To: 받는 사람의 이메일주소

8) CC: carbon copy의 약어로 동일한 메일을 수신자 외의 다른 사람에게 보낼 때 사용

9) BCC: Blind carbon copy의 약어로 동일한 메일을 수신자와 Cc에 적힌 수신자 모르게 제 3의 인물에게 보낼 때 사용

10) Subject: 주제를 밝히는 기능, 긴급한 내용일 경우는 'URGENT"를, 회신이 반드시 필요할 경우는 'REQ"를 적어 넣는다.

11) 첫인사: 무역서신과 대체로 동일하나, 상대방의 이름을 알고 있을 경우, Dear를 사용하지 않고, Hi! Mr. Kim 혹은 Hello! David으로 시작하는 것이 일반적이다.

12) 행과 문단: 내용의 명료함을 위해 한 행(line)은 70자 내로 적고, 3-4행정도의 문단 (paragraph) 사용이 적적절하다. 한 행이 70자를 초과할 경우는 사용되는 소프트웨어에 따라 모니터 상에 한 줄로 길게 나타나는 경우가 있으므로 내용을 읽기 위해 scroll 해야 하는 불편함이 따르므로, 이런 경우에는 의도적으로 행을 바꾸는 것이 바람직하다. 또한 이메일에서 영어 대문자를 사용하는 것은 때로 감정이 격해졌다든지 혹은 소리를 지르는 것을 의미하므로 조심해서 사용한다.

13) 끝인사: 이메일에서는 Yours, 혹은 Goodbye, Take care와 같은 표현을 사용한다.

14) 서명: 서명란에는 서신과 동일하게 handwriting으로 서명할 수 없으므로 송신자이름, 직위, 전화번호, fax번호, 주소, e-mail 주소, 홈페이지주소들을 적어 넣는다. 요즘은 software에 따라 서명 기능이 있는 것도 있다.

참고문헌

노승혁 (1997) 현대무역실무. 법경사.

추창엽 (1998) 무역실무. 형설출판사.

Brieger, N. & J. Comfort (1994) Early Business Contacts. Prentice Hall International English Language Teaching.

Colin-Jones, G. (1994) The Complete Asian Letter Writer, 3rd edition, Times Books International. Singapore, Kuala Lumpur.

Gartside, L. (1981) Model Business Letters, 3rd edition, Macdoland & Evans.

Gartside, L. (Revised by S. Tayler) (1992) Model Business Letters, 4th edition, Pitman Publishing.

Thompson, K.G. & D.S. Bland (1980) A Guide to Letter Writing, Pan Books Ltd, Cavaye Place, London.